Steeling the Mind of America

Steeling the Mind of America

Hal Lindsey
John Ankerberg
Henry Morris
Chuck Missler
Don McAlvany
Compiled & edited by Bill Perkins

New Leaf Press

First printing: June 1995

ISBN: 0-89221-294-2
Library of Congress: 95-69891

The information and opinions contained in each speech transcript reflect the views of the individual speakers and in no way are particularly endorsed by the speakers as a group.

Dedicated to Hal Lindsey, Chuck
Missler, John Ankerberg, Henry
Morris, and Don McAlvany

*...to whom so many owe so
much!*

Contents

Introduction

"My country 'tis of thee,
sweet land of liberty."

Words from the past and a challenge for the future.

A growing number of Americans believe that this country is veering dangerously off the course that was so brilliantly set by her founding fathers, just two centuries ago.

Conceived by the brightest minds and founded on the most noble principles, America has been called the greatest experiment in the history of human governments, and for the greater part of her history, America has recognized her place as a nation under authority to God.

But things have changed. The Supreme Court has now ruled that schoolboards cannot even mention the name of God. Deception has been substituted for truth, and humanistic philosophies are stealing the minds of people throughout America.

But truth stands, and thinking people, armed with truth and answerable to God, are the best hope for the future of our country and the guardianship of our families.

It was this concept, shared by a handful of people, that sparked the first Steeling the Mind of America conference. A play on words, the idea was to "steel" or "brace."

Against the deceptions that steal the truth, the most knowledgeable speakers were brought together to cover a wide range of issues, with a singular purpose — to uncover truth.

And the premise proved correct. Several thousand people attended the first two conferences and returned to their communities with extensive information and a greater understanding of what is happening behind the scenes. Tapes and videos from the conference had to be ordered and re-ordered to keep pace with the demand, as more and more people strive to get information they can't get from the controlled media. And finally, the decision was made to compile all the information from the first two years into a book so that it could be easily disseminated in one simple format.

We hope that it will be beneficial to you as you take an active part in navigating the future of America. Most of all, where there is deception, we hope it will "steel" your mind for the truth.

— Bill Perkins

1

The Battle for the Heart and Mind of America

John Ankerberg

In the 1860s, America was engaged in a Civil War. It pitted North against South, neighbor against neighbor, brother against brother. It was a war over this question: Would the slavery of black human beings be allowed or would there be freedom for all people? In 1860, Abraham Lincoln borrowed a phrase from our Lord when he warned the nation, "A house divided against itself cannot stand. This government cannot endure permanently half-slave and half-free. I do not expect the union to be dissolved. I do not expect the house to fall. But I do expect that it will cease to be divided. It will become all one thing or all the other."

Both of Lincoln's predictions came true. Our nation did survive, though it was tested to the point of near destruction and the death of 600,000 men. Equally significant, one view prevailed to the exclusion of the other: Slavery was wrong and could no longer be tolerated.

Today, another great civil war rages throughout America. Two sides, with vastly different and incompatible world views, are locked in a bitter conflict that permeates every level of American society. But instead of fighting with guns and swords, for territory or military conquests, this is a war fought with ideas for values and morality. It is a war for the hearts and minds of this generation of Americans. Soon, a winner will emerge and the loser will fade from memory. But the winner will decide how our civil laws are written, what our moral codes will be, how the family will be treated, and what values and beliefs our children will be taught.

Let's look closely at this civil war that's going on in our country. I want you to see the clear delineation of the two sides that are clashing. On one side, you have those who are called the traditionalists, those who hold to traditional values, the Judeo-Christian world view. These ideas have been dominant for over 2,000 years, and until recently they were dominant in our culture. What is the Judeo-Christian world view? It's the group that believes that God exists. They start with that assumption. God exists, and because God exists, certain ideas about how we live are derived from that belief.

For example, the value of man. The Bible says that God has created every man in God's image. This means we're valuable. We're not only valuable because we've been made in God's image, but God says we're going to be given eternal significance. The decisions we make are not just for this life, but for eternity. Man is valuable; he has an eternal value that God has given to him.

Also, the traditionalists believe that there are absolute standards of right and wrong. They also believe in lifelong marriage between male and female. They believe in the bearing and value of children, and that children are important. They believe in the dignity and value of the work ethic, the principle of common decency in society, and the value of education that teaches our young people God-centered moral values. All these flow out of the Judeo-Christian world view that starts with the assumption that God exists; He's there.

On the other side, the clash today is with those who could be called the secular humanists, the ones who believe that there is no God that we have to ultimately answer to. Now, what are the ramifications of their beliefs? They believe that there are no transcendent values. There is nothing that stands over time, there is nothing eternal. We just live for the moment, and that's it, and that moment doesn't have any significance. The only thing that's significant is what you or any other person thinks at that moment.

Right is determined by what seems right at the moment — not any absolute standard. And the standards that seem right today can change tomorrow. Or in the next moment. Since human beings have not been created in the image of God, you and I are not valuable. We have no eternal significance. The value of our life is not special. We actually have as much value as a drop of water, a rock, a plant, or anything else that you see on the earth. That's why the folks who embrace this view can also embrace infanticide, euthanasia, and abortion. Why? Because at some moment the life that exists can take precedence over the other life. There is no real value given to life.

Concerning sex, the secular humanist believes there is no right or wrong. Whatever sexual preference you desire, go with it.

The definition of the family is under attack. It wasn't too long ago in San Francisco's City Hall, a group of people put a petition before the local government of the city because they wanted to change the definition of marriage and family. The existing law limited marriage to only two persons at a time, male and female. They instead wanted the law expanded to include situations where two or more males or two or more females join together, and have these also be called a family. Fortunately, 10,000 churches got roused up and voted that one down. But, they will try again in the future to change the definition of family. It's still under attack.

These are the two sides: The humanists who believe that God doesn't exist, and the traditionalists, those who believe in the Judeo-Christian world view. And they are at odds. A fight to the finish in our country. Which group holds the power positions in the country? The most influential centers of power are held by the humanists. The universities, the news media, the entertainment industry, the judiciary, the state and federal bureaucracies, big business, medicine, psychology, law, sociology, the arts, our public schools, the halls of Congress — they're all heavily influenced by the secular humanist view.

Which centers of power are left for those who hold to the Judeo-Christian world view in our society? There are only two left: One is the Church. And the Church doesn't seem like it's up for this battle. The Church seems like it's lost taste for fighting for things it holds dear. The second one is the family. But the family is under attack. The family is under attack by being taxed, by being redefined, in our educational halls. It's being attacked there by our own teachers. If we've only got two power centers left, the Church and the family, what's going to happen to our culture if they fall? Let's look at what America will be like if we continue down this path of diminished influence from God and family.

In 1980, a California court ruled in the case of Kurlander versus Bioscience Laboratories that a mother must have an abortion if medical science indicates that her child will be born with a serious birth defect. The judge stated that failure to do so would allow the child to sue his parents for damages in later years. Believe it or not, that's what the judge ruled. Thankfully, about a year later, the California legislature reversed this decision in passing the Civil Code Section 43-6 to prevent handicapped children from suing their parents for permitting birth to occur. But from this ruling and other developments handed down in other courts, we can predict that in the future, in other situations, humanists will argue for forced abortion in order to control family size. This policy has already been instituted in China.

In China, where 63,000 children are born every day, abortion has become an important component of the government's one-child-per-couple family planning policy. Fourteen million Chinese women terminate their pregnancies every year.

The Chinese policy of permitting only one child per couple is openly applauded in this country by the liberals. They seem to be not the least disturbed that forced abortion has led to the deaths of millions of first-born babies who were unfortunate enough to be born female. This policy of forced abortion has already led to other problems in China. Reuter's News Service reported on February 21, 1990, there are now 689 single men for every 100 single women in China.

A second example of what life will be like under the humanist agenda comes from the American Bar Association's prestigious journal, *Family Law Quarterly*. An article published in 1988 with the help of an associate dean and professor of law at Georgetown University Law Center called for the licensing of all parents by the state. Unlicensed mothers and fathers would be required to give up their children for adoption. The authors admitted that the system could be used against parents whose ideas of child-rearing and family life are not in line with community standards. Here they have in mind anyone who thinks that homosexual or lesbian marriages are wrong, or who thinks the state has no business telling parents how to raise their children.

But for really cloudy thinking, in 1985 the Internal Revenue Service ruled that if a child is intentionally aborted, but somehow manages to survive for two or more days before dying, he can be declared a dependent by the parents who attempted to kill him. Follow the logic. The unborn child is aborted at his parents' request. But they are not charged with assault because he is not deemed to be human in the eyes of the law. But if he lives at least two days, he becomes a dependent for tax purposes because he is a child. But if he then dies a few hours later, his killers will not be charged with murder because he isn't a child.

This is pure secular humanism in action! When man abandons the wisdom of God and substitutes his own self-centered ideas, this is the illogical result.

How will the definition of marriage and family change if the no-God position wins? The answer has already been given. In an actual letter sent by the American Civil Liberties Union to the California State Assembly Education Committee, the ACLU stated that, "Monogamous, heterosexual intercourse within marriage as a traditional value is an unconstitutional establishment of a religious doctrine in public schools." In other words, the ACLU holds that anything that we have traditionally held in this country, if it emanates from the Judeo-Christian world view, is really religious and therefore unconstitutional and illegal.

But on this basis, one would also have to hold that belief in the Declaration of Independence and the Constitution of the United States is illegal. Why? Because in these documents, we find statements based on biblical teachings such as "We hold these truths to be self-evident, that all men are created equal and endowed by their Creator with unalienable rights."

Here's one other example of what America will be like if the no-God side wins. A father, dying of kidney failure, artificially inseminated his 16-year-old daughter with the help of her physician. Seven months into her pregnancy, the child was taken from her uterus by Cesarean section. The newborn baby's kidneys were removed surgically and transplanted into the father. Then the innocent new infant was cruelly left to die of uremic poisoning. If this sounds like something more likely to have occurred in Nazi Germany, it would be helpful to remember that the Nazis also made up their rules as they went along. Today, what seems right is right, we are told. These examples are not isolated horror stories. Rather, they are prime examples of many situations taking place today that help us to understand the liberal humanist mindset and identify its future objectives.

It's happening in our country and it's actually

worse than what we're presenting. If you want to read more, there are several books I would recommend. Good old Francis Schaeffer predicted this would come and how we should then live. Mel and Norma Gabler, in defending the Declaration, talk about how our country was founded on principles that we no longer adhere to in *What are they Teaching our Children in School?*[1] Robert Dugan, the NAE executive for Washington, DC, wrote *Winning the New Civil War.*[2] I recommend *Children at Risk*[3] by Dr. James Dobson and Gary Bauer; *Christianity and the Constitution*[4] by John Eidsmoe; and *The Cloning of the American Heart*[5] by Dr. Ronald Nash. This is where we have gotten our statistics and some of our illustrations. They are excellent books and they document what's happening in our country.

But let me take something that's a little easier to understand. Let's take a benchmark of 1960-1990, because most of us were living during that time. What's changed in our country? Let me give you one example, in terms of the public schools. This illustration might be familiar, but let me state it again. Do you know what the top offenses were in the public schools in the 1960s? This was listed by school teachers in their magazines. The number one problem was talking. Number two was chewing gum. Running in the halls. Wearing improper clothing. Making noise in class. Not putting paper in the waste basket. Getting out of turn in line. Those were the problems.

In 1991, they came out with a new list. Instead of just seven, they listed 20 categories. But consider the categories of problems that our schoolteachers face in the public schools in this country now, in just a 30-year swing of time. Number one: rape, then comes robbery, assault, personal theft, burglary, drug abuse, arson, bombings, alcohol abuse, carrying of weapons, absenteeism, vandalism, murder, extortion, gang warfare, pregnancy, abortions, suicide, sexually transmitted disease, lying, and cheating.

What's happened? We used to teach kids that God existed. It used to be okay to put the Ten Commandments on the wall. Now it's against the law to do that. And we're seeing the results. It's very interesting that the people in our country see no connection between what you teach a kid intellectually and how he acts. They don't catch that at all.

But what else has changed in America? Let's look at some other categories. In 1960, everyone knew that a family meant a husband and a wife with or without children. The law in 1960 was clear and precise in defining the family as people related by blood, marriage, and adoption. Most politicians at that time knew that any effort to strengthen the family was a good idea. But today, politicians can't even agree on what a traditional family is, or whether it is worthy of special assistance. There is a major movement underway to redefine the family to mean any group of people which merely thinks of itself as family. But then, would three men and a woman who think they are a family be a legal family? Doesn't that get us into the old problem of polygamy? What would this do to children?

Concerning religion in everyday life: In 1960, children routinely began the school day with a simple prayer or a moment of silence. At Christmas it was common to see a nativity scene near City Hall. Public service ads on TV urged families to attend church together on Sunday. A city billboard could read, "The family that prays together stays together." But today, in the 1990s, militant secularism prevails. Any public display of religion, whether a prayer at a high school commencement or a cross on top of a firehouse is immediately attacked by civil libertarian attorneys.

Concerning teenage pregnancy: In 1960, out-of-wedlock pregnancy was a matter of shame. When it happened, couples usually got married so that the child would have a name and the influence of a father. Girls who slept around were often ostracized by their fellow students. But in the 1990s, one out of five babies born in America was conceived out of wedlock. In Washington, DC, illegitimacy rose to an alarming 55 percent. Today in most public schools, the virtuous girl is considered odd and is subjected to scorn and ridicule. Surveys reveal that many of our sons and daughters are embarrassed to admit that they are virgins.

Concerning homosexuality: In 1960, it was still in the closet. The psychiatric profession treated homosexuality as a mental disorder or dysfunction. No politician could survive the disclosure of being a homosexual. The notion that special civil rights should be granted to people on the basis of their sexual orientation was considered an absurdity. Today, homosexuality is no longer considered a mental disorder or dysfunction, but rather an orientation, or a sexual preference. If you oppose homosexuality or condemn it from a moral perspective, you risk being labeled homophobic, a sickness described as a fear or loathing of homosexuality. Gay politicians celebrate their homosexuality and are routinely re-elected. Even a homosexual congressman who allegedly seduced several male pages was returned to office. Massachusetts Congressman Barney Frank, who admitted paying for sex with a male prostitute, received a slap on the wrist by his fellow congressmen.

Concerning our American heritage: In 1960, students in every American classroom began their day with the Pledge of Allegiance to the flag. History books widely used in the schools explained the religious heritage of the nation and were peppered with stirring illustrations of America's heroes and heroines. Our universities had a solid core curriculum that taught the classics of western civilization. Students were expected to be familiar with the great writers and philosophers of our culture as well as our Judeo-Christian heritage. But today, in the 1990s, the burning of the American flag has been designated by the Supreme Court as a form of free speech protected by the Constitution. In many American cities, the Pledge of Allegiance was not repeated at all or was suspended after the first few years of school. Many children today are deprived of any serious exposure to American history. When a school does offer history courses, they often present a revisionist viewpoint that emphasizes America's sins and failures rather than our forefathers' contributions and triumphs. Our universities can no longer agree on what every educated American should know. The works of the classical writers and the thinkers of our culture have been dropped from many university curricula and have been replaced with the rantings of Third World ideologues and revolutionaries. Even great institutions like Stanford University have jettisoned western civilization as a major focus of their curricula.

Now in any major conflict between two established armies, a bloody collision will occur that proves to be decisive. For Napoleon, the turning point was Waterloo. It was Stalingrad and Normandy for Hitler. It was Midway for the Japanese. Today the hottest and most dangerous confrontation to date in this civil war over values is being fought in the public school classroom over child and adolescent sexuality and the policies relevant to it. It is here that the secular humanists have made their most audacious invasion of the homeland. It is here that every cherished ideal and belief in the Judeo-Christian system of values has been assaulted. And it is here that slumbering traditionalists have awakened to find themselves surrounded and their children captured by the amoral views of the other side.

Look at what has been lost in just a few brief years. Virginity is now a joke. Pre-marital sex is the norm. Ten and 12 year olds talk openly about oral sex and the most intimate adult subjects. Dial-A-Porn has invaded their childish world. Homosexuality has become a valid lifestyle, with protected minority status. Traditional teachings of the Church are contradicted daily in the classroom. Parents have lost the right even to know when their daughters have aborted babies. Condoms are distributed by school officials. Venereal diseases are rampant. Language is so foul it is even criticized by the secular press. Why is it that the secular humanists have chosen child and adolescent sexuality in the public schools as the battleground on which to press their advantage? The kind of sex education program now operating in America's schools is designed as a crash course in relativism, in immorality, and in anti-Christian philosophy. What is at stake here is nothing less than the faith of our children.

And finally, we must ask what has happened in our society as a result of these sex education classes in the last 20 years. "Recent studies show that over 50 percent of all 15 year olds have had sex. This is compared to 10 percent 30 years ago. By the age of 19, over 75 percent of all young people will have lost their virginity. One in 10 girls will get pregnant before they finish high school, a total of over one million a year. Thirty to 40 percent of all sexually active young people are infected with one or more sexually transmitted diseases. There are now over 30 varieties to choose from. Several are incurable and at least two are fatal."[6]

The reason I focus on these facts is because I want you to get mad. It's only happened in 30 years. If we don't do something, what's going to happen in another 30 years? There are repercussions that are affecting us already. Every day, according to the statistics, 1,106 teenagers in the United States have an abortion. Every day, 135,000 teenagers carry a gun to school. Every day, 10 teenagers in those schools are killed by other teenagers carrying those guns. Every day, 54 teenagers in the United States are infected by AIDS, 378 a week. Every day, six teenagers in the United States commit suicide.

But let's look at crime on another avenue through some recent statistics. In 1992, 2.2 million Americans were physically attacked at work. An additional 6.3 million were threatened while working. There is a one-in-four chance that you or someone in your household will become a victim of crime in the next 12 months. Every year we now have in the United States more than 3.8 million burglaries. Twenty-seven percent of all American households are affected by crime every year. When you go to church, just count off the people in the pews. Every fourth family coming to your church has experienced a crime in the last 12 months.

What must be done if we're to reverse all of this? We've heard a lot about the bad news today, so let's change it for a moment. We say that we have the truth. We say that we're right, that truth will make our society something that we want, not the horror that we're starting to see. Well, what must we do? If we're going to get into the battle, if the battle can still be won, what must be done?

All Christians have been called by God to be watchmen, to warn the world of what God says. In the past, America has honored God. Our value system has emulated the biblical command. But now, can we seriously expect God to overlook America's sins because of our nation's past good behavior? The answer is no. In the watchman passage in Ezekiel, God warned, "I have said the good man will live, but if he sins, expecting his past goodness to save him, then none of his good deeds will be remembered. I will destroy him for his sins" (Ezek. 33:13). So if America does not turn away from its sin and rebellious ideas, God's judgment will fall upon us.

What can be done if we are to escape God's judgment and win the great civil war over values? First, we must awaken a sleeping army to fight. And we must realize that too many times we ask people to fight for traditional values before persuading them that this position is based on truth. People who are thinkers will not fight for a world view until they have carefully considered the evidence for the truthfulness of that view. Almost all traditional values are biblical values. But who is demonstrating that biblical values are true? Why should people believe that God really exists? Who is providing the evidence that Jesus is God? Who is proving that the Bible is the will of God revealed to man? Our purpose is to present and defend the evidence for biblical Christianity across the country. It is an appeal to thinking people.

Second, if we are to escape God's judgment and win the great civil war over values, we must not only realize that the biblical message is true, but that it calls us to commit ourselves to that truth. It means the acceptance of Christ as Saviour and Lord, and it means living under God's revelation. Christians should be ashamed for not proclaiming this message, because only the Christian world view supplies true reasons for moral values and gives real meaning and purpose to life. But if people who claim to hold the Christian world view do not enter the war to fight for what we believe, then we're going to lose everything by default, and the humanist side will control the nation and have access to training our children.

The fact is, we can start to reverse this if we will get involved. As we said before, the Church seems to be like a sleeping army. Why is it that the Church sleeps? Why is it that you can go into town after town and the people won't get involved on any of the social issues? Francis Schaeffer gave the best illustration before he died. He quoted from the Old Testament, and said, "Do you remember Hezekiah the king? Isaiah came to him and said God had given him a message to give to the king. And it was a devastating prophecy. It included the fact that a foreign power would come and invade Israel. This foreign power would capture Hezekiah's kingdom and carry away his children. What if somebody said that to you about your household, or your business, or your church? What would you say? Do you remember what Hezekiah said? The Bible says, Hezekiah remarked 'If this is what the Lord wants, it is good.' In other words, whatever the Lord says is okay. But then the Bible goes on to say what he was really thinking in his heart. He said, 'At least there will be peace and security during the remainder of my own life.' In other words, as long as Hezekiah could live his life in peace and security, he didn't care if up ahead at the end of his life, the nation was destroyed and his children were captured."

Isn't that exactly what's going on in America today? People, as long as they have their own peace and their security, their own money, their own job, are not going to get involved. And for the most part, Christians have been left untouched until now, but it's changing. I read that passage 10 years ago and thought to myself, *I wonder if there will ever come a day when God will remove the security of American Christians.* What if God removes our wealth? What if God takes away that job of yours, your business, and there are no jobs? What if God takes away your savings account or the money that you do have in your savings is absolutely worthless? Could it happen? In a heartbeat.

Several years ago, a friend of mine by the name of Larry Burkett sent me the galley of a new book called *The Coming Economic Earthquake.* I'm not into economics, but I read that book and I thought, *There's a ring of truth to that book.* That was a stunning book.

The second thing that got my attention about our finances in this country occurred when I went to Congress and actually started interviewing congressmen. I found out they agree with Burkett. That really shocked me. Since that time, a new crowd has come into Congress, and a lot of new things have happened.

Clinton was supposedly elected to balance the

budget and reduce the national deficit. When he was trying to get NAFTA passed, he needed one more vote to get it passed. He bargained with Senator Bob Kerrey. Kerrey said, "I want you to take a look and have a special committee appointed of congressmen and senators to investigate the national debt." Clinton says, "You give me your vote; we'll do it." Kerrey gave him the vote. Clinton then appointed a 32-member blue-ribbon panel to investigate the national deficit and entitlement program. On August 9, 1994, they gave their first report and it said that by the year 2012, 17 years from now, unless immediate policy changes are implemented, 100 percent of all the taxes that the government collects from all Americans will not be enough to pay for just two categories: the interest on the national debt — not the principal, just the interest — and for the entitlement programs that are currently in place. In other words, 17 years from now, according to Clinton's own panel, we'll be broke.

The panel didn't stop there. They reported that currently it takes 60 percent of all the taxes, of all Americans, just to pay the existing entitlement programs and the national debt. By 2000, just a few short years from now, the Medicare hospital insurance fund will be insolvent. By 2010, the baby boom generation will begin to retire and three years later there won't be any money in Social Security. This is not the conservatives talking. This is Clinton's liberal committee. Bob Kerrey responded, "This tells us that we're on the road to bankruptcy."

Now it's important that they issued that warning first. They were supposed to make their recommendations of which areas to cut so that we wouldn't go bankrupt in that period of time. But Clinton signed a bill delaying that part of their report. Why? Because before they could make recommendations to the Congress of which entitlement programs to cut, they first had to debate the granddaddy of all entitlement programs, Social Security, that George Mitchell says will cost us $1.1 trillion in 10 years being added to the national debt. This is idiocy.

So Clinton's panel concluded that the country will be broke in 17 years. Here are direct quotes from some influential people, from live-to-tape interviews at the 1994 Steeling the Mind Conference.

"I believe that we're facing a crisis, an economic earthquake, if you would, that can destroy the finances of most Americans — destroy their retirement plans, their Social Security income, their bank accounts, their insurance companies, and their jobs, if we're not very careful. Now that sounds alarmist, and I'm not an alarmist. All I'm doing is dealing with the facts and figures provided to me by the U.S. government, and those facts and figures are really alarming. Before the end of this decade, we're facing a situation where the government cannot pay its bills, cannot even pay the interest on the bills that are already owed." (Larry Burkett, Christian financial adviser)

"The national debt does matter when you consider that if we don't do anything about the debt in cutting the deficit, then our spending habits, we could have a debt anywhere between $15-$20 trillion by the year 2000." (Congressman Tom Delay, Texas)

"Here's a problem with the national debt. We are right now paying $1.4 billion each day on interest alone. All that money could be spent on penal reform, health care, education, wherever you want to put it, or most especially go back into taxpayers' pockets, but right now, it's just going on the interest. We came up here to cut the debt. It's right now at $4.4 trillion. After the Clinton budget is in place for five years, it will be over $6 trillion and it's just totally out of hand." (Congressman Jack Kingston, Georgia)

"During the four years of the Clinton presidency, the budget deficit is still going to grow by $1.3 trillion. We're going to owe $1.3 trillion more than we do right now." (Congressman Richard Pambo, California)

"We're adding $15,000 per second, $879,000 per minute, $52.7 million per hour and $1.27 billion per day. That's the increase in the national debt this year. The total is $480 billion this year added to the national debt. We've never seen anything like this in our history. Spending is out of control." (Congressman Bill Dannemeyer, California)

"If you compound the rate of interest growth, combine that with the government overspending, it's already guaranteed that somewhere around the year 2000, we have about a $13 trillion national debt where no matter how much you tax America — maybe you tax them at 75 percent of their income — they couldn't keep it current. Then what happens? You run out of money as a government. And the government starts to print money." (Larry Burkett)

"We are very near to losing it, to reaching a point of irreversibility. Because I'm an optimist, I say let's fight. Let's not let our parents and our grandparents down. Let's not let our kids and generations yet unborn down. Let's hang onto the American dream." (Congressman Robert Duran, California)

Clinton's committee said that in order to keep pace, by the year 2007 we would have to increase taxes 87 percent.

At the same time we ponder the national debt, we hear economists say, "Look, as long as the economy is growing, you can still have your debts grow." But the problem is, what if the economy is not growing? With the new taxes and the new regulations on business, we are losing jobs and the fact is the very economy, the engine that is paying for all of the social programs, is being destroyed.

There are so many areas to pursue, but I'm going to touch on one more area that involves the new environmental regulations on business today. I interviewed some of the leading environmental scientists in Washington, DC, and one of them is Dr. Fred Singer, who was in charge of the EPA for many years. Now he's in one of the think tanks in Washington. I also interviewed one of the professors from the University of Virginia who talked about one specific problem — global warming. Right now, the government is taking action to avert what they call global warming. But what's the cost? And is the problem a real problem? There are trillions of dollars in tax money that are going to be poured into curing this problem, and it's going to be at the expense of millions of American's jobs. Does the problem really exist? That's what we want to talk about; consider what a couple of the most well-known scientists in Washington said:

"Let me see if I can put it as succinctly as possible. Unless we bring some balance back into this environmental issue that's going on in America today, there will be no industry in America in the next century. It will be impossible to start up a new business that has any pollution, and it will be impossible to operate a business that has any pollution. It doesn't mean that those industries won't exist; it means they're going to migrate out of this country into other countries. Unfortunately, that is the environmental agenda. In fact, if you take it a step further than that, the extreme environmentalists would like to apply the same rules and regulations to every country of the world and basically, in order to have a zero-risk environment where nothing is polluting, you shut down all industry." (Larry Burkett)

"When I was attorney general of the United States, we tried to vigorously enforce the law that was necessary to protect the environment, to protect the health and safety of the people. But we did it in a common-sense way, and we did it on the basis of proven scientific facts. Today, unfortunately, there's a very different approach." (Edwin Meese III)

Now there are many illustrations of how our

government has rushed in to create expensive environmental regulations to correct problems that many scientists believe do not even exist. Global warming is just one of those problems.

"It impresses me, the level on which these environmental activists think. I'll give you an example. They have now convinced our Congress and our President that there is a global warming problem. And that this problem is so severe that we have to buy into a program to lower carbon dioxide emissions in America, back to 1990 levels at a cost of about $2 trillion and about 2 million American jobs because they think the environment is getting warmer and we're going to melt the polar ice caps and we're going to flood the world." (Larry Burkett)

"On global warming, I'd like to make a major point here. That is, the public thinks that scientists all think alike. They've been told that there's a scientific consensus about global warming. They've been told by some politicians that 98 percent of all scientists believe that a global warming catastrophe will occur in the next century. That's just not true." (Dr. Fred Singer)

"The problem with the greenhouse effect is if you believe these forecasts of gloom and doom, and I do not believe them based upon the data, then you have to impose a level of command and control on the individual's life which will make any past regulation look very, very small." (Dr. Patrick Michaels)

"There have been all kinds of calculations — theories, mind you — calculations based on theories as to what the increase in carbon dioxide and methane will do to the climate. By now, you know the increase over the pre-industrial value of all these greenhouse gases combined, has been about 50 percent. Yet we don't see any effect. We don't see anything in the record that shows a warming. The models, the calculations predict that the warming in the next century when the gases double will be five degrees, plus or minus. So we should have seen by now a two and a half-degree increase. We don't see it. In fact, the best data we have, taken from satellites — these are data that measure temperature all over the world, very precisely, with a very good instrument, a single instrument so there's no question about calibration or comparison or being disturbed by ground activities — show no change in temperature whatsoever over the last 15 years, contrary to what all the theories predict. What does that mean? It means that there is something wrong with the theories." (Dr. Fred Singer)

"I have come to the conclusion from looking at the data on the global warming issue that the gloom and doom scenario simply does not stand up. Now, if we're going to have a policy to stop something that's not occurring, that's not going to be a very good policy. It's not going to be underpinned by the facts." (Dr. Patrick Michaels)

"This is just an environmental myth, in my opinion, supported by the extremists, and its ultimate goal is the same: control. They want government in control of industry, of lives. And if this thing goes through, and it looks like our government's on the track to put it through, we're going to eliminate millions of jobs and we're going to see tens of thousands of businesses in America shutting down and moving to countries that don't have these silly environmental laws that we are now creating." (Larry Burkett)

Why is this happening? Because we haven't gotten involved. These policies have been passed while we've been living in the last 30 years. People who have been active for their agenda have gone into Washington and they have continued to pester the politicians until they've gotten little-bit by little-bit passed. Now, we're going to pay for it. We still have a chance to be heard. Talk to people, read these things, find out about the policies that are being passed.

But where is the Church? As Hezekiah said, "As long as my own peace and security is not touched, it's okay" (see Isa. 39:8). The country could be damned in the next generation and our Christians are sleeping and refuse to get involved. We have got to change that. They are starting to pay for it via crime, via what's happening in the schools, via what's happening in their taxes, and it could bankrupt the country very shortly unless we get involved now.

What will happen if we compromise further? Listen.

Today, many people are willing to compromise most everything as long as they can live their own life in peace and security. In fact, many Americans currently act very much like British Prime Minister Neville Chamberlain, who on September 30,

1938, signed the Munich Peace Pact with Hitler. That pact gave the illusion of peace and safety, but it cost Czechoslovakia its freedom and ultimately brought all of Europe into a great conflagration. Only Winston Churchill discerned what was happening and sounded the alarm. His words to the House of Commons could just as well apply to millions of compromising traditionalists in America today. Churchill declared: "The people should know that we have sustained a defeat without a war. They should know that we have passed an awful milestone in our history and that the terrible words have for the time being been pronounced against the western democracies, 'Thou art weighed in the balance and found wanting.' Do not suppose this is the end. This is only the beginning of the reckoning."

Like Churchill, I believe that God has weighed our country in the balances and found us wanting. Now we've just got a few short years for the Church to wake up and to act. If we don't, that will be it. The war will be over and we will have lost. Could it happen that quickly?

Friends, yes it can. We've seen what's taken place in 30 years. Let's look at another country, England. Many people do not realize that in the 1940s and during the war, England was deeply religious. Perhaps 60-70 percent of the entire population went to church every Sunday during those years. The people thanked God openly for rescuing their nation during the war years.

Today, less than three percent attend church in

England. What changed? They allowed humanists, people who believe that God doesn't exist, into the schools to teach the kids, and they raised an entire generation that turned away from God — didn't even know about God. In one generation the war was over. And now there are no debates about abortion in England. There are no debates about homosexuality. There are no debates about the traditional values that we hold dear. Why? Because the war is over for England. It's also over for countries such as France, Germany, Holland, and Belgium. The traditionalists lost because they didn't speak out.

Could it happen here? We now have a generation that's being raised in our schools where they don't hear about God. It's against the law to have the Ten Commandments put on the bulletin board, even to mention the name of God, to have a Bible on a teacher's desk in front of the class. We are currently raising a generation that's going to be the same as England. They won't even know about God. What's worse is that right now we even have adult Christians who are starting to believe the lie that this country wasn't founded on Christian principles; they're starting to believe this newspeak that's coming across America that the founding fathers really didn't believe in God, they really didn't put this country on a biblical basis. To show you how wrong that is, I'd like to review a few historical facts.

Our founding fathers expressed their beliefs when they wrote the Declaration of Independence and said, "We hold these truths to be self-evident that all men are created equal, that they are endowed by their Creator, with certain, unalienable rights." It was during the troubled Constitutional Convention of 1787 that Benjamin Franklin rose and addressed the delegates and said, "In the beginning of the contest with Britain, when we were sensible of danger, we had daily prayers in this room for divine protection. Our prayers, sir, were heard and they were graciously answered. All of us who were engaged in the struggle must have observed frequent instances of a superimpending providence in our favor. Have we now forgotten this powerful friend, or do we imagine we no longer need His assistance? I have lived, sir, a long time, and the longer I live, the more convincing proofs I see of this truth, that God governs in the affairs of man. And if a sparrow cannot fall to the ground without His notice, is it probable that an empire can rise without His aid? We have been assured, sir, in the sacred writing that except the Lord build a house, they labor in vain that build it. I firmly believe this. I therefore beg leave to move that henceforth prayers imploring the assistance of heaven and its blessing on our deliberation be held in this assembly every morning."

In George Washington's first Thanksgiving proclamation, he admonished, "Whereas it is the duty of all nations to acknowledge the providence of Almighty God, to obey His will, to be grateful for His benefit, and humbly implore His protection and favor." As he concluded his presidential term, he said, "Of all the dispositions and habits which lead to political prosperity, religion, and morality are indispensable supports." John Adams succeeded Washington as our second president. In 1775, he wrote, "It is religion and morality alone which can establish the principles upon which freedom can securely stand. A patriot must be a religious man."

During the Civil War, President Abraham Lincoln urged all Americans to participate in a national day of prayer with these words: "We have been the recipients of the choicest bounties of heaven. We have been preserved these many years in peace and prosperity. We have grown in numbers, wealth, and power as no other nation has ever grown. But we have forgotten God. We have forgotten the gracious hand which preserved us in peace and multiplied and enriched and strengthened us, and we have vainly imagined in the deceitfulness of our hearts that all these blessings were produced by some superior wisdom and virtue of our own. Intoxicated with unbroken success, we have become too self-sufficient to feel the necessity of redeeming and preserving grace, too proud to pray to the God that made us. It behooves us, then, to humble ourselves before the offended Power, to confess our national sins and to pray for clemency and forgiveness."

President Woodrow Wilson said, "The Bible is the one supreme source of revelation of the meaning of life and the spiritual nature and need of men. It is the only guide of life which really leads the spirit in the way of peace and salvation."

One final question remains: Where did the

phrase, "the wall of separation between church and state" originate, and what does it mean? First of all, the author of the Bill of Rights was James Madison. He also authored the First Amendment with its religious clause. He eventually became our fourth president. What did he think the First Amendment meant? Madison wrote, "Before any man can be considered as a member of civil society, he must be considered as a subject of the Governor of the universe." After Madison had written the First Amendment, he served on the congressional committee that recommended the chaplain system for congress.

It was 11 years later, in 1802, that President Thomas Jefferson interpreted his understanding of the First Amendment to the Danbury Baptist Association of Connecticut. The terminology Jefferson used in his letter about the "wall of separation between church and state" came to be accepted as what the Constitution implied. What did Jefferson himself think, and how did he imply his own concept? In 1803, only a year after the Danbury letter, as president of the United States, Thomas Jefferson made a treaty with the Kaskia Indians in which he pledged federal money to support their priests and to build them a Catholic church. Later that year, Jefferson sought funds from Congress to finance the obligations of that treaty. It's more than mildly astonishing that the author of the "wall of separation" concept asked Congress to fund religious activity in his own time. It is therefore unthinkable that Jefferson would have allowed the American government to forbid political activity motivated by religious values.

Today, if Christians read the words of our founding fathers, then they will not be afraid to fight for the implementation of biblically based moral principles in this country. In doing so, they will find themselves in the distinguished company of the founding fathers of America.

2

Seven Keys to Watch in Bible Prophecy

Chuck Missler

It's disgusting that we have to prepare ourselves against widespread deception but it's coming from almost every direction: newspapers, television, radio, magazines, our government, and even our schools. True professional analysts invariably retreat to foreign media and specialized newsletters to find out what's really going on in the world, and even here in our country. One of the questions that arises is, "Where is the media in all of this?" Many have had the opportunity to review the video called *The Clinton Chronicles*. The most shocking disclosure in that entire series of interviews was by Don Hewitt, the executive producer of "60 Minutes." He admits that "60 Minutes," airing on a major network, purposefully withheld the truth from the public in order to patch Clinton up so he could win the New Hampshire primary. Our long-trusted media prostituted its mandate for the truth for what you might call political correctness. I call it deception.

White House legal counsel Vince Foster's death is another example. Christopher Roddy did a thorough analysis and highlights 40 discrepancies, and yet the media won't air it. To get the truth these days you have to know somebody on the inside, or search the foreign media. If you regularly subscribe to the *Economist* or the *London Sunday Telegraph*, both respected European publications, you get the unfiltered truth about what's going on in Washington. Incredible information you won't find in our own media. Why?

In America we have traditionally relied on the media to be informed and uncensored, something desperately needed to protect the stewardship of our votes. It's very troublesome to discover that you simply cannot trust the mainstream media anymore. Deception is not just negligence or laziness; it appears to be well-planned, with some very devious intent.

If we're analyzing statistics, we typically take a look at certain trends and assume that the past is an indication of the future. One of the conceptual mistakes we all make is to presume linear assumptions in a world that's very non-linear. We all tend to take for granted that tomorrow will be like yesterday. We do it instinctively. And yet when we stop and think about life for just a moment, we realize that life is very non-linear, there is a great discontinuity. We find it in the natural world; nature is that way. We call them floods. If you ask someone in the Midwest about floods, he'll tell you about it. If you want to talk about hurricanes, ask somebody from central and southern Florida. If you want to talk about fires or riots, talk to someone from southern California. Those are non-linear events.

Politically, the Berlin Wall came down. Politically, how many of you have noticed changes in the former Soviet Union in the last few years? These are non-linearities. In our personal life, we're constantly confronted with non-linearities. A death in the family, etc. One of the things that we're not prepared to think about are non-linearities on our national scene. We tend to presume that tomorrow in this country will be like yesterday; and yet we look around as we begin to realize that as we examine the evidence, there are a lot of changes.

Einstein Knew It

But there is something even more fundamental, another conception that I'd like us to try to outgrow. That is this concept of time. Our conception about the concept of time is linear and absolute. We all presume it is. For thousands of years philosophers have presumed this peculiar dimension we call time is linear and absolute. Part of this comes from our schooling; we all had to go to the blackboards when we were kids in school and draw what they call a time line. We drew a line from left to right on the blackboard. The beginning of the line on the left was typically the birth of a person or a nation. The right end of the line was typically the end, or terminus, of a person or a nation. So we think of time lines.

Because of those types of experiences, when we encounter the concept of eternity, we naturally imagine a line that starts at infinity on the left and goes to infinity on the right. Therefore, when we encounter the concept of God, we imagine someone who has lots of time. But all of this turns out, interestingly enough, to be bad physics, thanks to the insights of Dr. Albert Einstein. He had the perception to realize that we live in a four-dimensional universe. Three spatial dimensions plus time. He recognized that time is a physical property. We now know that time changes with mass, acceleration, or gravity. If I have an atomic clock and I raise it 100 meters, it speeds up by one part in 10 to the fourteenth. Not enough to change your schedule, but it's something that's profoundly significant — that time is a physical dimension.

The National Bureau of Standards put an atomic clock on an airplane going around the world eastward. It lost .06 microseconds. They put an atomic clock on a plane going around the world westward and it gained .27 microseconds, exactly the amount predicted by Einstein's equations. If you take a course in physics, you'll always run into the hypothetical twin astronauts. Two guys born at the same instant; one stays on the earth, the other is put into a spaceship and sent to the nearest star, Alpha Centauri. This star is about four and one-half light years away and back, at about half the speed of light. When he returns, he's two and one-half years younger than his twin brother. That example is just a way of getting across the idea that time is elastic. Time is a variable. Time is a physical dimension.

Now the question you want to think about: Is God subject to gravity? Is God subject to the limitations of mass or acceleration? Hardly. You see, God is not somebody who has lots of time; God is somebody who is outside the dimension of time altogether. That's what Isaiah meant when he said "the high and lofty One that inhabiteth eternity" (Isa. 57:15;KJV). That's what God meant when He said, "I make known the end from the beginning" (Isa. 46:10;KJV). Now if God had the technology to create us in the first place, He certainly has the technology to get a message to us. The question is, how does He authenticate it? How does He let us know the message is really from Him?

I come from a technology background. I spent my executive career primarily in the high technology industry. One of the two great discoveries in my life was the discovery that these 66 books that we glibly call the Bible, penned by 40 authors over thousands of years, is an integrated message system. Every number, every detail, is there by design. An integrated, singular message system, and very demonstrable. You can demonstrate that it has its origin from outside the time domain. God has authenticated His message by writing history in advance.

We could talk very colorfully about hundreds of examples where the Bible predicted history before it happened. But today you and I have an exciting opportunity. We are being plunged into a period of time about which the Bible says more than any other period of time in human history, including the time that Jesus walked the shores of Galilee and the mountains of Judea. So that makes this whole premise, this whole preposterous, strange, bizarre idea I've just expressed empirically verifiable.

So you really don't have a big philosophical issue, but rather very simple answers. Number one, you need to learn what the Bible says about these things. That enables you to sit back and watch it unfold. But, you have no chance of understanding the news, what's going on, unless you know your Bible.

There are seven major areas everyone needs to watch.
• **Babylon**

In Isaiah 13 and 14 and Jeremiah 50 and 51 there are passages that describe the destruction of the city of Babylon. Most of us have been taught that it occurred in 539 B.C., except, if you do your homework, you discover that's not true — despite the many well-intentioned Bible commentaries. Babylon was *conquered* in 539 B.C. by the Persians; it was not destroyed. It became a secondary empire. The Bible describes the *destruction* of the city of Babylon. This is the pride of the Chaldeans on the banks of the Euphrates, the literal city of Babylon. Yet it describes its destruction in terms that have never happened.

What does that mean? Well, for one thing, it means the libraries are full of expositors over the centuries who have argued whether that passage is to be taken literally or figuratively. Maybe it's allegorical.

The reason I'm bringing this up is that for the last 20 years, Saddam Hussein has been rebuilding the city of Babylon. Now the reason that's so provocative is that if the Bible is to be taken seriously, the city of Babylon has yet to be destroyed the way the Bible describes it. There have been debates for centuries about whether those passages are literal. Today it's academic because you can go over there and take a look. You may only need a one-way ticket, but you can go over and take a look at the Processional Way, the Ishtar Gate, the temple. Take a look at Saddam Hussein's summer home on the bank of the Euphrates. (The Euphrates has moved a little bit, but not a lot.) The point is, Babylon is there, now. You can say, "Well, those are just some ceremonial buildings." That's right. The palace of Nebuchadnezzar — it was described in Daniel 5, the handwriting on the wall, and all that — is there. Saddam Hussein spent hundreds of millions of dollars, even getting the best archaeologists to validate the foundations before building it. He uses it for affairs of state. To anyone who's secular, the real action — especially during the Persian Gulf War — is in Baghdad. Not for you and me. The action for you and me is 62 miles to the south — literal Babylon. Now, it's just a few buildings, but that's the interesting point that I want to make. You can look at it today and disparage and say, "That's not very significant." The Bible says its going to emerge as a major power center and be destined for destruction. That's an exciting example, because it gives us an opportunity to sit back and watch. Skeptics or believers, do your homework so you'll know what it says, and just watch and see.

• **Israel**

If you really want to find out what time it is on God's calendar, always look at Israel. And of course, there's always a lot going on in Israel. There's always talk about the PLO. I'm one of these who tend to dismiss it as nonsense. Why? Because the PLO does not speak for Israel's enemies. The PLO was going broke until the U.S. bailed them out of trouble by making them prominent in the peace negotiations. Israel's enemies include the Hezbollah, the Hamas, and 13 other groups. Violence has increased since the latest peace accord, not decreased.

But there's something else going on that's even more interesting. That's the treaty with Jordan. The Bible says in Daniel 11:41 that this region that we call Jordan is one of the few regions on the planet Earth that escapes the rule of the Antichrist, apparently to provide a refuge for the remnant that will flee Israel at the right time. That is biblically significant, and the fact that that relationship has surfaced is something we do want to watch.

What's the next step for Israel? That's an easy answer — the rebuilding of the Jewish temple. The first temple, built by Solomon, was destroyed by the Babylonians. The second temple, built after the return to the land, became remodeled to be what we call Herod's Temple. It was there when Jesus walked the earth. Then it was destroyed by the Romans in A.D. 70. For over 1,800 years there has been no temple, no altar, no acceptable sacrifice for the Jew.

We know that the temple is to be rebuilt because in the New Testament, Jesus, Paul, and John make reference to it. What's exciting right now is that the Temple Institute in Israel has built 63 of the 93 implements required for service. They have 200 young men in training to be priests in that temple. Scientists are scanning the world for the right marine snails to yield the levitical blue and the royal purple for the very vestments that are presently being woven in linen on semi-automatic looms. It's all coming together. They're getting ready to rebuild the temple.

There are three possible sites. The traditional site is under the Moslem "Dome of the Rock," a mosque built over 1,000 years ago. For many technical reasons, this being the actual site to rebuild the temple is dismissed by most technologists. Dr. Asher Kaufman published research about 10 years ago arguing some very good reasons why the temple appears to actually have been slightly to the north of the Dome of the Rock. But the most exciting news is that the temple actually stood about 100 meters to the south of the Dome of the Rock. I have received infrared photographs that prove the real Wailing Wall is actually about 40 meters inside the current location. The Israeli scientists are closing in on the details as they prepare to rebuild.

They obviously can't rebuild until the political situation is quite different. At the moment, the Temple Mount area is controlled by the Moslems and they are not motivated to give up any of it — especially to the Jews, whom they hate. I don't want to get into all the conjecture about how that's going to unfold, but we do know it's going to be built. The Bible says so. Jesus, Paul, and John make reference to it and the Israelis are getting ready.

We have put Israel in a military dilemma where their only option to survive may be a preemptive nuclear strike. I got an inside briefing at NATO headquarters in Brussels, and they admit that the thing they fear most on earth right now is a war in the Middle East because they realize that the next one will probably be nuclear.

• **Russia**

Ezekiel 38 and 39 discuss in fine detail a still future battle, the famed invasion by Magog, the ancestor of the Scythians. We know them as the Russians. They invade Israel in the latter days, and lose badly. The more you study Ezekiel's passages in terms of its technical detail, and the more you know of the current intelligence briefings, the more you recognize that event could happen at any moment. The political subtleties are all in place. The principals involved in this battle are presently practicing the maneuvers. We watch them closely on reconnaissance satellites because we can learn what their strategies are.

As you should already know, Russia is more

dangerous now than it ever has been in its past — if for no other reason than the instability and the power-grabs going on. When the Soviet Union was in charge, we knew all the procedures that were in place to prevent an accident. They may have been very cold, very calculating, but they were rational. Today we've got an irrational turmoil in Russia, and I was shocked when the assistant secretary of defense, Robin Beard, and our ambassador to NATO, Robert Hunter, both admitted to me, off the record, that they don't even know who is in control of the button for launching nuclear missiles!

You may have heard a lot about Vladimir Zhirinovsky, this bombastic character who knows how to grab a headline. Don't totally write him off. The parallels between him and his autobiography and Hitler's *Mein Kampf* are interesting. Zhirinovsky's autobiography, titled *The Last March to the South*, reads like Ezekiel 38 in many ways.

There's something else I'll mention because most people don't realize it. Russian President Boris Yeltsin has signed a document which substituted a new symbol for the Russian federation. The hammer and sickle of the old Soviet Union is gone. But what is the symbol of the Russian Federation as of January 1, 1994? Yeltsin established what many would consider the most unlikely symbol you can imagine — the Romanoff double eagle of the czar. This was the Russian symbol from 1472 until Nicholas II was assassinated in July 1918. Of course, anything having to do with the aristocracy was taboo for 70 years.

Using this type of symbol is very uncharacteristic in recent Russian history.

The Romanoff double eagle is a gold eagle on a red background, and it has a shield in front with a rider riding a white horse. The double eagle faces east and west; it was the symbol of the Byzantine Empire until Ivan the Terrible adopted it for Russia. That's the new symbol of Russia today.

What you also might notice is that the name of the parliament was changed to the duma, which was what they called it under the czar. Why am I getting into all of this? When Yeltsin visited Spain a few months ago he secretly visited a young count. This gives rise for some speculation that one of Yeltsin's strategies might be to reestablish a constitutional monarchy. The argument would be that a 1,000-year-old monarchy may have more legitimacy than a four-year-old democracy widely viewed as a failure. If this happens, some of the estimates are that the Russian Orthodox church and the army would rally behind it for stability. We're certainly not trying to make any forecasts here, because in Russia even the past is uncertain.

This classic scenario in Ezekiel 38 and 39, which describes nuclear weapons, both in terms of their source of energy for Israel for seven years and in the after battle nuclear clean-up procedures, is very graphic.

Magog, in Ezekiel 38 and 39, invades Israel with a band of allies. In verses 5 and 6 of that passage you have a list of the allies. The lead ally is Persia.

Today, we call it Iran. And, of course, you're quite acquainted with the fact that Iran is the strong man in the Middle East. It's spending about $5 billion a year on its air force. Iran is armed to the teeth. Rafsanjani has at least seven nuclear weapons and he doesn't have to buy them on the black market anymore. Russia has signed a treaty to be militarily affiliated with Iran and its intrigues. That was the price for Iran to keep its hands off Central Asia. Russia has also agreed to build two nuclear plants in Iran for nuclear research facilities.

Five republics broke off from the former Soviet Union and they all have three things in common: 1) They don't have cash to feed their people, but 2) they do have nuclear weapons, and 3) they're Muslim. It doesn't take a lot of imagination to see where many of the arms that the Middle East needs are going to come from. They'll come from their Muslim brethren.

• **Islam**

Most people in this country are misinformed about the origin, nature, and agenda of Islam. First of all, Islam did not begin with Mohammed. That's a common fiction promoted by many special interests. When Abraham was called out of Ur, the worship in that region was the worship of the moon god, which went by many names. In Arabia, Allah was known as Al Ela. Al Ela was the leader of 360 idols that made up the worship emphasis of pagan Arabia. They would march around Al Ela seven times, and then run three miles to throw rocks at the devil, all traditions that characterize Islam. In fact, Allah was their name for their moon god in the early years, and eventually god in general.

Abdallah was Mohammed's father. As he grew up, Mohammed synthesized this heathen practice into a monotheistic form. But it's still the worship of the moon god and that crescent moon still adorns every mosque on the planet Earth.

The Muslim faith is spreading rapidly. Eleven-hundred Christian churches in England that have been converted to mosques have that crescent moon on them. There are more Muslims in the United States than there are Jews. Don't make the mistake of thinking that Allah, as they would call him, is the God of the Old Testament. Allah is capricious. Read that "untrustworthy." As you go through the Koran's teaching on it, you'll realize there is no parallel, even in concept, with the God of the Bible. Islam is occultic, satanic, and it is Satan's instrument to attempt the destruction of Israel.

When you read the allies that are listed in Ezekiel 38, you'll be shocked to discover there's not an Arab among them. You can talk about Persia, Assyria, Iraq, Libya, Egypt, and Turkey, but they are not Arabs. You'll discover that the Arabs are, in verse 13, sitting on the sidelines, very nervous. Why are they on the sidelines? From the passage, you can't really tell, but we do notice today that Iran is practicing with its amphibious operations, under conditions of contamination. Now they don't have to do amphibious operations to invade Israel. What tips off that part of their strategy is the invasion of Saudi Arabia. No wonder the Saudis are nervous. The U.S. has spent over 10 years secretly arming Saudi Arabia. Why? First of all, why would Iran want to invade Muslim Saudi Arabia? Because they're Sunis, not Shi-ites. That's like the difference between the Protestants and the Catholics in northern Ireland, only worse. Saudi Arabia is also considered bad news in the Islamic world because they let us use their real estate in the Persian Gulf War.

Even more importantly, Rafsanjani of Iran has made several important announcements. One is that he believes Islam has replaced Marxism as the ideology of the future. He also believes they now have the resources to disconnect the Middle East from its Judeo-Christian world order. By resources he means cash flow from oil and nuclear weapons. Rafsanjani has also announced what he calls his grand design, the unification of the Muslim world, the roughly one and one-half billion followers all the way from Indonesia to Muritania. Also, watch closely the strange rapport that's beginning to develop between Islam and the Vatican. That's an interesting couple of bedfellows. The bottom line is that the Bible talks about Islam as a major player in the end times and we see that piece of the puzzle coming together as a perfect fit.

• **Europe**

The Bible predicts in Daniel 2 and 7 the most bizarre arrangement to occur at the end times. It predicts that the Roman Empire will re-emerge as the dominant political entity on earth. That gives rise to ancient scholars referring to this as the revived Roman Empire. I have studied this Bible prophecy passage for more than 30 years. I was in the board room of Ford Motor Company in the 1960s when they made their decision to build their business strategy on the basis that Europe would emerge into a super-state. What the Bible predicted has been coming, like a glacier, for the last several decades: Europe is re-emerging as a unified super-state.

When most people think about the Roman empire coming together, they think about the European Community, currently 12 unified nations. I'm not referring to them. In the so-called EC 12, there were six originally; six more joined them subsequently to make 12. *Another* six are joining them, so it'll soon be 18. (Don't say "six plus six plus six," it's not that easy.) And there may even be more nations joining in the future.

Regardless of the make-up, they will have a great impact on world trade and politics. They collectively have a population base of 350 million, compared to our 250 million. The United States has helped promote a unified Europe on the theory that we were going to build a capitalistic, pre-market, democratic trading partner. What we failed to realize was that we were helping create a protectionist, socialist, competitor. Europe has a gross national product larger than ours, their cost of capital is lower than ours, and their affection for us is not very encouraging. World War II was a long time ago.

A world-impacting treaty was recently signed

in Europe. Most people who follow international affairs believe it was the most important event of the century. Most people in America didn't even know it was happening. It's called the Maastrich Treaty, named after a town in the Netherlands where it was first drafted. It was signed by all 12 EC nations. This treaty provides, not for a federation of European states, but instead, a single, unified, European state with a common military, common foreign policy, and ultimately a common currency. Some people believe this treaty is so radical that it's going to come apart and create anarchy in Europe. That's possible. Others believe it's just another step to intense centralization and definite movement toward the fulfillment of biblical prophecy.

On a recent trip to Europe, I had the privilege of meeting with many key European government officials and noticed two consistent views about America. The first was that the ignorance in America is overwhelming. It's amazing how ignorant we really are as a people about our own affairs, let alone Europe. The second was that they feel the concentration of power in America is frightening. That bothered me. I considered myself a well-informed executive; I've spent the last 30 years orchestrating international deals, and it never occurred to me that way. The concentration of power in this country *is* frightening. Ask somebody, "What's the biggest problem in this country, ignorance or apathy?" And they'll say, "I don't know and I don't care."

France and Germany are now combining their

military. Have they no history books? France and Britain are building ships together. A common military emerging from all twelve. The symbol of Europe is Europa riding Zeus. You and I would describe it as a woman riding a beast holding a cup in her hand. That sounds exactly like chapters 17 and 18 of the Book of Revelation.

One World Government/New World Order

The real theme that comes out of all this is the movement towards globalism and a one world government. We see it in our country. Presidents Bush and Clinton have moved us that direction, aggressively. In Europe, they also believe there's going to be a one world government. I believe most thinking people, secular and Christian, take for granted there is going to be a one world government. They'll discuss ecology, population, world hunger, etc., never touching the real reason it's going to happen. The one world government will happen because there's no alternative. The reason is nuclear proliferation. There are over a dozen countries today with nuclear capability, and they all seem to be mad at each other. Also, there are over 23 countries today building inter-continental ballistic missiles. So it's just a matter of time.

Now the question is, "Why are we dismantling our military?" Suppose our military was built to 10 times its present size. What would you do with it? Who would you point it at? See, the problem is not that simple. The obvious answer is global supervision. Therefore, everybody takes for granted there's going to be a one world government.

The race is on for control of this world government. That's why they're pushing so hard in the U.N. They want to be in control. However, in Europe they have a different idea. They regard the U.N. as an American plaything, funded by the Rockefellers, domiciled on U.S. soil, whose track record is abysmal. If you read Daniel 2 and 7, you know that ultimately a superpower will emerge and it will be Europe-centered.

All of these areas I've mentioned are moving along the ancient scenario that was written in the Bible thousands of years ago. The Bible describes a period of time in which God is going to intervene in history and set up His own government. Bizarre idea. All of this will be associated with the second coming of Jesus Christ. The details of the events prior to that Second Coming are laid out in amazing detail. Now, you and I may disagree on some subtle details. But the point is that there are parallel themes well documented in the Old and New Testaments having to do with Babylon, Israel, Jerusalem, Europe, Russia, the rebuilding of the Jewish temple, etc. Not just one; all of them are unfolding before our very eyes. So the staggering conclusion you cannot escape is that it is coming to a climax.

What excites me most is that here is tangible proof the Bible means what it says and says what it means. God said that time itself is non-linear; it's going to come to a climax. The biggest non-linearity of all is about to unfold.

Now there is a problem because of a particularly American anxiety: "What about the United States?" As you look through the Bible, you see a climax with a four-power conflict we call Armageddon. It's triggered by a group called the "kings of the South" who are joined by "kings of the North," this western European confederacy, and a far eastern force. The main point is that there are only four forces mentioned. Where's the United States? There are many different views. None very satisfying.

The greatest nation the earth has ever seen is mainly conspicuous because of it's absence from the end-time scenarios. Some people feel we're simply aligned with one of the mentioned four groups. Possibly. But most analysts believe that by the time those things take place, the U.S. will be irrelevant. That's not a recent rationalization. You'll find those kinds of views expressed for many decades. Today they are very vivid. Let me tell you candidly, without getting into statistics, from my secular perspective. America, as we know it, is over. We are broke. We're existing only on our borrowing power. The month-to-month bills of the U.S. government cannot be paid by its cash flow; it has to do it by foreign borrowing. And the day will come when they feel the risk is not worth the investment. That's already visible by the devaluation of the dollar. Not in the last few months; the last 20 years. We're living beyond our means and the European bankers are getting tired of it. Soon they will cancel our credit cards.

I grew up in the forties. There's something

about those times I want to focus on. There was a morality in the air. I don't mean just nationalism. We were taking on a challenge in Europe. It was black and white, it was good and evil, and you could easily sign up to give your life for that battle.

Many of you may have read the saga of people like Bill Donovan and William Stevenson, the guys who set up the British Secret Service. They set up the headquarters in Manhattan, New York, because they feared Hitler would overrun Great Britain and they would have to regain the island from this country. But you don't realize unless you do some homework, they had no budget. The people who did that did it out of their own pocket. They did it out of a commitment to stop the tyrant in Europe. Different days.

Then came the fifties. Korea, a police action. A whole string of those kinds of things, which climaxed in a degrading sense with Vietnam. Unpopular wars, where fighting men felt like pawns of political winds of change. This gray, neither black nor white, era went from the fifties through the eighties. One thing I want to applaud today is the clarity. It's no longer gray. It's getting awfully clear who the bad guys are and who the good guys are. But if you listen to the liberal media, it's backwards — we are the bad guys.

A lot of people give me flack and say, "You're supposed to be running a Christian ministry and you're talking about politics." Not exactly. I'm not disparaging an interest in politics, but we're talking about something a little different. Let me ask a question: If someone accosts you in an alley with a gun and takes your wallet, do you feel that you've been plundered? Of course. Suppose you find out that it wasn't one guy. He actually had two or three partners. Do you still feel plundered? Has anything changed? You still lost your wallet. Suppose you find out it really wasn't three or four guys; it was several hundred. Does that minimize the degree to which you've been plundered? No. Suppose you find out that the robber represented 51 percent of the people in town. Does that change anything? It's plunder by any other name. The fact that he might even have a badge from the local jurisdiction doesn't change the fact that you lost the wallet.

Let me try another example. Suppose you and I and a third party decide to go to dinner. We decide we will each order and then split the bill three ways. There is a strategy open to you as to what you order, isn't there? Applying that kind of logic, suppose we agreed to have a credit card. And the three of us were just going to share a credit card and at the end of each month, we'll just divide the bill three ways. Can you see the problem? Now imagine having a credit card with, say, 500 people? All you've got to do is split the bill each month by 1/500th, and everybody is free to go order what he wants. Do you begin to see what I'm building? When you think these things through, you'll discover that socialism is theft. And the last time I looked at Exodus 20, I believe that's a commandment. Exodus 20 endorses private property; it says, "Thou shalt not steal."

What you also discover is that as you create

social ills, you also create government opportunities. You've probably noticed the whole pattern of declaring some kind of crisis to ramrod some kind of new erosion of your freedoms. What they've finally figured out is that there is a formula here. The more crises you have, the bigger your government can get. Government is always interested and owned. Citizens of every country in the world make a distinction between their country and their government. They love their country; it's their home. But they don't trust their government, because they recognize it's an enemy of their personal freedom. There's only one country in the world where the average citizen gets confused between his country and his government, and guess what country that is?

It finally became clear to me what the game is. If social ills create government opportunity, it doesn't take a lot of imagination to create more social ills. I suddenly figured out why the government has an incentive to promote immorality. Think about it. There have always been homosexuals. Long ago we had Sodom and Gomorrah. What was terribly wrong in Genesis 19 was that the people condoned it. It was the official policy. Our government promotes, endorses, and encourages immorality.

As you think this through, you'll realize something else. The whole concept of being an American was the concept that we have available God-given rights, not man-given rights. The rights we enjoy are God-given and it's the role of the government to protect them. Once you realize that, and you realize the opposite agenda of the government, you begin to realize why they've got to get the name of God out of our culture. As long as there is God and the rights are God-given, their hands are tied.

What is the goal? Why is this prostitution of our heritage going on? It gets back to global dominion. It's a race to control the world. If I read Daniel 2 and 7 and some other passages right, it's a race that the United States is going to lose. Some others are going to win.

I came across a quote by Samuel Adams recently that blew me away. His challenge was as follows: "If you love wealth better than liberty and the tranquillity of servitude better than the animated contest of freedom, go home in peace. We seek neither your counsel nor your arms. Crouch down and lick the hands that feed you. And may your chains rest lightly upon you. And may posterity forget that you were our countrymen."

In the Book of Amos, the northern kingdom of Israel was subject to four situations and conditions. First, they felt militarily secure — no one threatened them. Second, they felt rich — they had new trade routes and everybody lived in a nice house. Third, they worshipped idols — they forgot the God who brought them through the wilderness. And fourth, they forgot their heritage. God tolerated this situation for 160 years, and then finally sent the prophet Amos to call these things to their attention. Through Amos, God gave them an opportunity to repent. They didn't repent, and within 40 years of Amos' prophecy they not only went into slavery, but they were also eliminated as a political entity.

As I read the Book of Amos, I'm fascinated with the parallel. We think we're militarily secure, but we're in more jeopardy than we ever have been in our history. There are presently 12,000 missiles aimed at U.S. cities that are only 30 minutes away. We feel we're rich, and yet our government is beyond bankrupt, living its borrowing power, which is a very temporal thing. Do we worship the God upon which this country was founded? Hardly. We worship idols of all kinds. Make a list. We also have forgotten our heritage. Many people get upset, they say this whole concept of civil disobedience is always a sensitive subject. Let's not forget we're a representative republic; and it was specifically founded on the God of the Bible.

Many of us have what I would call Rapture-itis. It's a uniquely American disease. We have this idea that before things get really bad, we're all going to be out of here, so we're too concerned with our current situation. Don't misunderstand me. I happen to be very pre-trib, in fact, I'm pre-seventieth week of Daniel. But the question is, how certain are we of the timing? He could come in the next 2 seconds, next 2 hours, next 2 days, next 2 months, next 2 years, or maybe the next 20 years. Jesus said, "Occupy till I come." We need to make a distinction in our eschatology between the Great Tribulation, which is a specific period of well-defined persecution and normal persecution that has happened since Christ walked the earth. People tend to forget that most of the body of Christ, for the last 1,900 years, has been under severe persecution. To claim Jesus Christ, more often than not, subjected you to the penalty of death.

Do you have fire insurance on your house? Of course. Are you expecting a fire? Hardly. It's called prudence. It's just something you do as a good steward. What happens if things really fall apart in this country and the Lord's timing of His arrival is yet downstream a bit. We need to think about that. I will tell you candidly I do believe, from my knowledge of this country, that only a miracle can save America. The good news is that God is in the miracle business. I believe this country can be saved, but it will only be done in the prayer closet, not the ballot box.

I want to tell you about a place called Ninevah. Ninevah was 40 days from ground zero. And God called a guy by the name of Jonah to go preach to it. Ninevah had ruled the world for seven centuries. This place was sin city and Jonah wanted no part of it. In fact, Jonah went in the opposite direction until God explained His program a little more clearly. You know the story. But the greatest miracle in the Old Testament, in my view, is not Jonah and the whale, but the repentance of Ninevah. Because the king repented, and they got another hundred years respite because of that repentance. Yes, God's judgment may be on America, but God's judgment is never beyond repentance.

You and I are engaged in a spiritual warfare. But that term may be used too denotatively in your own mind. We often fail to recognize our adversaries. They often wear three-piece suits, carry briefcases, speak good English, and network effectively. Too many of us have sat by while they trampled our heritage, demeaned our God, and stole our blessed liberties. And I suggest we have no right to bemoan that which we did not fight to protect.

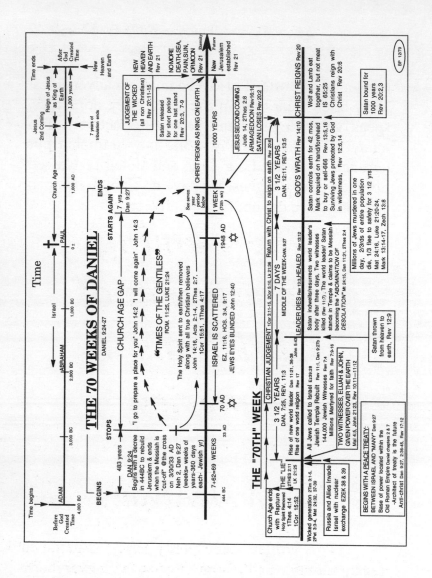

To receive a laser print of this chart on a full
8-1/2 x 11 sheet of paper, please send $2 to:

Compass
3115 North Government Way, Suite 800
Coeur d'Alene, ID 83814

3

The Coming Persecution of Christians in America

Don McAlvany

I've written some pretty heavy material in recent months, and it's not popular with everybody who reads it. I believe it is my mission, my calling in life, to push Christians from their comfort zone. But it's not easy telling people what they don't want to know. I have an intelligence-gathering background and have developed many contacts around the world. There are a lot of good people in the intelligence community and they are very frustrated about what they see going on behind the scenes: atrocities that the media will not, or cannot, report.

So, I report it.

The Political Spectrum

The political spectrum has been so garbled and confused by the political left in this country that we, as Americans, don't understand who is on the left, who is on the right, and who is in the center. On the far political left of the traditional political spectrum is a dictatorship, which is total control of a government by one person. Some examples of the political left would be communism, monarchy, fascism, secular humanism, and national socialism. Another name for national socialism is nazism. On the far political right is anarchy which is no government at all. No police, no restraint, and where mobs run wild in the streets.

The early politicians in the United States — Thomas Jefferson, George Washington, James Madison, Ben Franklin, etc. — were in the political center. They did not establish a democracy but instead they established a constitutional republic. They knew that a pure democracy would never survive in the long run so they formed a constitutional *republic*. In a republic, there are certain basic rights and guarantees given to minorities, regardless of the majority thinking. These founding fathers understood the excesses of anarchy from their experience in Europe. They also understood the excesses of dictatorship and monarchy and so they chose to establish a type of government that leaned to the political center.

This new constitutional republic called for three different branches of government: the legislative branch, the executive branch, and the judicial branch. These branches had checks and balances against one another. Most elected representatives in those early years were Christian in their beliefs and politically in the center.

Where are we today? In the last 20 years, the political left has redefined where the political center is. They say, "Look at the conservative, anti-Communists in the United States — they are on the far right." What the liberal media has done is take people who belong in the political center and positioned them to the right.

I'm a constitutional conservative. I believe in our traditional values. I believe in our traditional way of life. I believe in what George Washington, Abraham Lincoln, James Madison, and Ben Franklin believed. These men were not radical right-wing extremists. They were in the political center. But, by redefining where the political middle actually is, they've now put an inaccurate label on people who think like I think, and believe what I believe.

If George Washington were alive today, espousing his political views, he would be defined by the liberal media as a right-wing extremist and "politically incorrect." But he was not right-winged at all. Socialism and liberalism have been re-defined as the political center. This has resulted because we have allowed people with very liberal views to use the media to influence the bulk of Americans with incorrect information. The media has totally distorted and garbled the political spectrum. The media has been able to do this because of the tremendous influence they have and the fact we, as Americans, don't know our historical roots, nor do we know basic political science.

Parallels between the United States and Nazi Germany

When you study world history you'll find common denominators between nazism, fascism, and communism. All three are powerful, totalitarian, dictatorial governments which control all aspects of their subjects' lives. Massive numbers of rules are characteristic of all three. Regulations and laws are enforced by an all-powerful bureaucracy. All three have a common pre-occupation with death. All three are based on man's reason and a rejection of God, His authority, and His law. Socialism, which America is moving toward at break-neck speed, is simply communism or nazism minus the total dictatorship. Socialism is a very small step away from communism, or nazism.

As a leading Communist and the head of the labor socialist party, John Strachey said in England in the 1930s: "We can't have a direct transition from capitalism to communism; we've got to use socialism as a stepping stone, so all of us Communists should be working for socialism." Lenin, Stalin, Hitler, Mussolini, Gorbachev, Castro, and Daniel Ortega, all were, or are, Socialists. And, unfortunately, most of what Bill and Hillary Clinton are advocating —

national health care, gun control, etc. — is socialistic.

Let's look at some interesting parallels between the United States and the Third Reich. Most people condemned the Nazis because of their external manifestations — the extermination of millions of Jews and other death and destruction of World War II. But nazism was more than just killing Jews and starting wars.

Preoccupation with Death

First and foremost, in Nazi Germany they had a tremendous preoccupation with death. In the United States we terminate 40 percent of the pregnancies in America by killing the babies. Forty percent! Ninety-eight percent of abortions in America fall under the category of birth control. Since *Roe v. Wade* there have been 30 million deaths due to abortion. But they terminated a higher percentage of pregnancies in Nazi Germany in the late 1930s and early 1940s.

Euthanasia is becoming legal through the efforts of Dr. Korvakian and the sympathetic liberal media. Germany was also into euthanasia. Adolf Hitler instructed his top doctors to implement euthanasia on a large scale. Over 274,000 old, sick, crippled, and mentally ill people were killed during a span of about three years. The Nazis had a major pre-occupation with death and so does the United States.

Rejection of God's Ultimate Authority

In Germany, they rejected God, His authority, and His law. Is it any different here in the U.S.? Much of the shift toward the left in America has taken place because evangelical Christians didn't take an active stand for what they believe. Few of us take the time to write a letter to our congressman asking them to vote against using federal funds for abortion. Fewer help staff a crisis pregnancy hotline. And very few of us pray daily for the leadership of this nation. It's taking its toll.

These are just some of the many reasons why I believe God may be close to judging Christians in America. In fact, our country may be moving under God's judgment right now. Consider what's going on all around us: destructive weather patterns, the AIDS problem, new social diseases, a 50 percent divorce rate, a looming depression, potential economic collapse, and a relentless assault on Christian values and freedoms. It's easy to see that the prosperity which we've all taken for granted in this country may be coming to a screeching halt. Even solidly established personal freedoms are being carefully dismantled by a government which seemingly desires to control every aspect of our lives.

The average kid grows up watching far too much television. From age 3 to 19, the average child will view approximately 20,000 murders or crimes of great violence. Twenty thousand!!

Occultic Emphasis

There was an occultic dimension in the Third Reich. The leaders in Hitler's hierarchy were heavily into the occult. Many of them were Satan worshippers, including Adolf Hitler. This is one of the reasons there was tremendous anti-Semitism. Also, many people don't realize they were not just killing Jewish people, they were also killing Christians. Whenever you see a rise of witchcraft, satanism, and the occult, you always see a tremendous turn against fundamental, evangelical Christianity and against orthodox Jewry.

Gun Control

We were given the right by our Constitution, in the Second Amendment, to hold and to bear firearms to defend our country, to defend our homes, to hunt, etc. Our founding fathers, George Washington, Madison, Adams, and others, set up our country this way for a reason. In the countries where they took the guns away from citizens, the citizens lost their constitutional powers. This happened in Nazi Germany. Germany instituted special gun laws. Laws that eventually disarmed their population. We, fortunately, still have the constitutional right to bear arms — but for how long? Piece by piece we are losing the right to bear arms. Every thinking person knows that guns don't kill people, people kill people. Guns are not the problem.

Animal Rights

Nazi Germany had a pre-occupation with animal rights. They went bonkers over their animals. It became a crime to kill an animal. They passed laws against killing barnyard animals as well as against hunting game. They even passed laws covering the boiling of a frog or the boiling of a lobster. Now these are the same people who could kill men, women, and children by the millions and yet they would weep over the death of an animal. What an incredible inconsistency. They were killing people without remorse and shed tears over animals. Sound familiar?

Let's look at America today. We have people who worship planet Earth and its animals, who believe that you can put hundreds of thousands of people out of work to protect the snail darter, the spotted owl, wolves, whales, or whatever. These are the same people who believe there are too many people in the world and want population control through abortion and euthanasia. It's hard to understand that kind of an inconsistency unless you see the occultic, satanic dynamic behind it.

Historical

Germany had a great constitution. But the German people ignored it. We are ignoring our Constitution today. Our judiciaries, our Congress, and our presidents are running roughshod over the Constitution. They're running roughshod over our constitutional right to due process, personal freedoms, and guaranteed rights.

Germany had a great heritage. Remember, they gave us Martin Luther. But they ignored their heritage. Today we are not only ignoring our great national heritage, we are allowing our educational system to totally erase it. Our public educators are rewriting our history, taking out all references to Christianity. This despite the fact our nation was founded on biblical principles by dedicated Christian men who openly served and acknowledged Jesus Christ as their

Lord. They are removing references to our Christian heritage despite the fact that over 80 percent of the quotes from our founding fathers before 1820 contained scriptural references or references to God.

Homosexual Rights

In the 1930s in Germany, there was an open homosexual community for the first time. We have not only an open homosexual community, we have allowed it to have tremendous influence in the lives of Americans. This despite the fact that the Bible calls a homosexual someone in sin and a pervert.

Abuses of Power by Elected Officials

Don't forget, Adolf Hitler was elected to power — elected! There was no coup. In less than 15 years Germany went from a respected, strong country into political, financial, moral, and spiritual decline. Are we in that same kind of decline here in the United States? "Woe to those who call evil good and good, evil" (Isa. 5:20;NIV).

Everything we're talking about in this move towards a socialist America can be described in four words: to control the people. People-control is the center to any totalitarian state, whether in Nazi Germany, the former Soviet Union, Cuba, or in trying to socialize America in the 1990s.

Increased Regulations

In Germany, they had thousands of laws, rules, and regulations passed in a short period of time. Laws that covered everything. There were so many laws that the Nazis could finger anybody they wanted as a criminal. New categories of crimes were created while criminals themselves were being given lighter and lighter sentences. The U.S. government passes tens of thousands of new regulations each year. In 1992, there were 67,700 pages of new laws passed in the U.S.

Most of these new laws carry both criminal and civil penalties for violation of them. To implement these new laws, tens of thousands of new regulations were written by over 100,000 government bureaucrats who were part of dozens of huge government agencies: the IRS, the SEC, the ATF, the BATF, EPA, OSHA, HUD, etc. These new regulations, many of which carry criminal penalties, filled 67,700 pages of the Federal Register in 1992. You, as an American citizen, are responsible for following every one of those regulations or risk possible fines, asset forfeiture, or imprisonment for violation. Ignorance of the law in America is no excuse. You have been legally advised via the Federal Register.

Government regulations, according to Thomas D. Hopkins, Rochester Institute of Technology, are now costing us over $600 billion a year. You eliminate those regulations, and many of those regulators, and you've eliminated a major portion of the U.S. deficit.

Incredibly, the government has created a situation in which you are almost certain to be doing something that could classify you as a criminal; you're probably breaking one or more of these regulations right now and don't even realize it. That's the same tactic used in Nazi Germany. You could take anyone sending money out of the country and accuse them of violating the financial laws, the monetary laws, or the exchange control laws. That was Nazi Germany. Could it happen here? They never thought it could happen there.

What about all the new environmental regulations? Most everyone will agree that there is a pollution problem — at least in the major cities. But by passing the Clean Water Act, the Clean Air Act, and a host of other environmental laws and regulations, the government now has new, far-reaching controls over virtually every business, person, piece of private property, and car.

I believe that the environmental laws and regulations, both domestic and international, will be the primary vehicle for moving the U.S. toward socialism and the New World Order. Seventy percent of private real estate in America can be interpreted by the government to be a "wetland."

Do you understand what a wetland is? The government defines wetlands as any area that has water in or around it! Most people wrongly assume that a wetland area has a river in it, a lake, pond, stream, marsh, or a swamp. Not so. A wetland could be out in the desert. By having the authority to designate property a wetland, they can tell you what you can and cannot do with your private property.

Thousands of U.S. citizens or businesses each year are being fined, having their property seized, or even jailed for wetlands violations — most not having a clue they had done anything wrong.

Socialists many times will use a crisis, real or manufactured, to expand their power and control over people. Here in the United States we have "the war on drugs," "the environmental crisis," "the war on crime," "discrimination against minorities," "war against hate crimes," "firearms violations," etc. All are "crises" which supposedly justify the passage and enforcement of new laws and regulations with new levels of bureaucrats.

In recent years we have heard of the "child abuse crisis." Most people don't understand the government's definition of child abuse. It's not just beating or sexually abusing children. The government defines child abuse as spanking a child. In fact, there are people who have been jailed in different parts of the country and lost their children because they spanked their child and a teacher or social service worker found out about it. The U.N. Convention on the Rights of a Child, which the United States supports, claims that one of the primary forms of child abuse is spanking children.

The way things are moving, if you teach your children that the Bible says homosexuality is sin and wrong, you will not only be committing a hate crime, and a civil rights violation, but also child abuse.

In the book *Putting People First*, by Governor Bill Clinton and Senator Al Gore, on page 72, paragraph 2, calls for a national police force of 100,000 to fight the "crime war" and other American "crises."[1]

Are they talking about the child abuse crisis, the gun control crisis, or the environmental crisis? We've never had a national police force before. Nazi Germany had one. The Russians had one. The Red Chinese have one and the Cubans have one. I'm all for the FBI doing the traditional things they've always done, and the CIA chasing spies, but anything even resembling a national police force makes me nervous. Whatever happened to our local police and our local sheriff's departments? They're supposed to keep the peace in our cities and states — that's what's in our Constitution.

The New World Order crowd is also talking about an international police force made up of U.N. troops from member countries to control internal crises, environmental abuses, and potentially, opponents of the New World Order. The New World Order U.N. police force will soon reach 100,000 and could grow to 250,000 or more over the next five years. Do you know that U.S. troops are now serving in the U.N. international police force? That's never happened before. We've never had our boys serving under foreign commanders. Not until right now. Could U.N. troops be used in America in some future civil unrest such as riots or other upheaval?

Local, state, or military helicopters, with greatly increasing frequency, are overflying cities, towns, neighborhoods, and individual's houses at low levels looking for drugs, etc. These helicopters are unmarked and usually have people photographing houses, etc. Why? I believe they're all part of an umbrella group called the Multi-Jurisdictional Task Force, which may actually be the new name for the national police force.

Government Extremes

Over the past two years, confrontations with Americans who are characterized by the government as religious fundamentalists have been widely publicized. Let's look at some recent examples.

• **Randy Weaver**

You probably wouldn't agree with some of his religious views, but I do believe he is a born-again Christian. As a resident of Idaho, he was approached by a couple of government agents, and they said, "We want you to spy on your neighbors and tell us which ones have guns."

Weaver had a lot of friends in Idaho, and he said, "No. I'm not going to do that. I think that's wrong. I can't believe you would ask me to do that."

And as the agents left (from trial transcripts), they said, "We will come back and we'll get you." And about six months later, without Weaver realizing who they were, a couple of undercover agents befriended him. This is called an underground sting or undercover sting. After a while, they asked him if he'd buy them a couple of shotguns. And he did. What Weaver didn't realize was that he had been set-up. One of the shotguns was a quarter of an inch too short and therefore illegal. The undercover agents then charged Weaver with federal firearms charges. Weaver actually claims that they weren't too short when he had them, that they had sawed them off later. But, even if they were too short, the normal punishment would be to fine him.

Wanting to tell his story to the judge, a trial date was set. But, before he got to trial, he got an anonymous tip that said, "You don't have a chance. They're going to railroad you. The testimony is all stacked against you." And so he did what many country boys would do, he ran to the hills with his family. He spent the next year and one-half with his family, home schooling his kids, studying the Bible. They farmed, and he even ran for sheriff.

Then one day eight federal marshals, dressed in federal ninja suits, came onto his property with fully automatic weapons. The Weaver family's dog ran out and barked at the agents, and they shot the dog dead. Their 14-year-old son Sam ran out to see what was happening, and saw that his dog had been shot. He turned around, started to run for the cabin, and they shot him in the back, four times, killing him instantly.

Weaver and another man named Kevin Harris came running out. They grabbed the boy's body. Harris fired one shot in the direction of the one who had just shot Weaver's son, killing a U.S. marshal. (There seems to be some question as to whether the marshal could have been killed by Harris or by so-called "friendly fire," but no one will probably ever know.) Hundreds and hundreds of federal agents were surrounding the place. That started the "Siege of Ruby Creek" that lasted for 10 days.

On the fourth day an FBI sniper from Quantico, Virginia, had been called in. Apparently they had done a computerized profile of the family, concluded that the wife was the strong suit, and if they took her out, the siege would end. On the fourth or fifth day of the stand-off, Randy Weaver and Kevin Harris snuck out of the cabin to pray over the body of Weaver's dead son. As they came back into the cabin, Weaver's wife, Vicki, holding nine-month-old baby girl Elisheba in her arms, opened the door about a foot to let them in. The FBI sniper shot her between the eyes, killing her instantly. The baby dropped to the ground. Blunt bone fragments injured both Weaver and Harris who had just come back in the cabin. Weaver had lost his wife and a son.

A very highly decorated policeman from Phoenix, Arizona, got onto the property and was able to finally talk the guys out after 10 days. Immediately, the three children, a 9-month-old child, a 9-year-old girl, and a 14-year-old girl, were charged with murder and conspiracy. Of course, Weaver and Harris were also charged with murder. The national publicity pressured the government into dropping the charges against the children.

The trial lasted for several months. During the trial, according to the judge, the government was caught lying over and over. The government prosecutor walked out of the courtroom, and never came back. The defendants were ultimately acquitted of all charges except some misdemeanor charges. Is that due process?

• **Donald Scott**

Donald Scott was a millionaire living in Malibu,

California. He owned several hundred acres of very valuable ranch land. The government had approached him several times to buy the land but he said he didn't want to sell it. One morning about 7:00, as he was sleeping in bed with his wife, his front door was splintered open. Thirty agents, most of them dressed in black ninja suits with either automatic, semi-automatic, or fully automatic weapons, came charging through the door. His wife jumped up to see what was going on. The intruders grabbed her as she was coming down the hall and threw her down on the floor. The agents then ran into the room where Scott had been sleeping. Not knowing who was invading his house, he pulled a pistol out from underneath his bed. (Is that such an odd reaction?) They told him that they were government agents so he raised his hands. They then told him to drop the gun. If you've used guns, you know you don't drop a gun from six or seven feet high. So he leaned over to put the gun on the ground, and they shot him six times in the chest, killing him instantly.

The assistant district attorney for the city of Los Angeles was a good friend of Donald Scott. He wrote a 100-page report in which he said this was simply a cold-blooded murder of an innocent man by the U.S. government. The agents apparently came in to try to find drugs so they could confiscate or seize the property. What did that man do to deserve to die in his own home? Exactly what crime had he committed?

• Waco, Texas

Few people really understand the whole story of Waco. In fact, most would like to forget it. But, just exactly what did those folks, in what *Newsweek* called "the killing ground," do to deserve to die? *Newsweek* said David Koresh had a death wish, and maybe he did, but that's no reason to kill him.

Koresh came out of a Seventh-Day Adventist background. Most people would disagree with their religious beliefs although I don't think we'll ever know what they actually believed. The media described them as a "dangerous religious cult." These people had been in Waco for a long time and as far as we know, they hadn't broken any laws. They had been investigated for possible violations but never charged. They had been accused of child abuse and Texas Social Services had been in the compound on three separate occasions and could find absolutely no evidence of child abuse. They had been investigated for gun-control violations and had actually been taken to court. The county sheriff came out and served them with a warrant. They went to court and the court said, "There's nothing illegal here," and their guns were returned.

About six months later, 100 agents of the Bureau of Alcohol, Tobacco, and Firearms surrounded and attacked the Koresh home. They said they were just trying to serve a search warrant and go in and see if there were any illegal guns.

Before, when they had served the warrant, Koresh let them in and they searched the premises.

But this time the agents surrounded the building and charged, with guns blazing and throwing stun grenades in the windows. On the original charge, three BATF agents were killed.

Eventually, 8 or 10 Branch Davidians were killed that day, and the Waco siege began. The BATF was relieved by the FBI to complete the operation. Koresh was stupid and should have come out. Who knows what was going on in their minds? Maybe they were frightened. Don't forget, out of nowhere, dressed in all black attire, scores of agents charged their building and killed 10 of them. Maybe that scared them.

On the fifty-first day, the government launched an attack at about 6:00 in the morning. Fire departments and several fire trucks had been on hand throughout the 51-day siege. But they were sent away before the attack started and they were not allowed to return until an hour and one-half after the flames had broken out. Why would they do that?

The FBI launched the attack by punching holes through the building with tanks. This is strange behavior in a building where you've got 24 or so kids, women, and elderly people. The BATF said, "Well, we had no choice. We couldn't get Koresh." What do you mean, you couldn't get Koresh? He used to jog around the neighborhood all the time. He was out buying groceries and going to the cafe. They could have grabbed him anytime they wanted. This is not the way you serve due process; this is not the way you serve a search warrant, not according to the U.S. Constitution.

Then they started pumping in CS gas. Janet Reno, Bill Sessions (who was head of the FBI), and Bill Clinton said, "It's just a harmless irritant." Give me a break. I served in the military. I know what CS gas is, and any of you who served in the military and have done police work know CS gas is 80 times stronger than tear gas. It is a war-time, battlefield, chemical warfare agent. We used it in Vietnam to flush out the Viet Cong. It would immobilize them, they would fall to the ground, they would go into convulsions, and they would be deathly ill. Sometimes they would die. In fact, there have been reports that some children could die of this. You throw up, you go into convulsions. You can't walk; you're totally immobilized. This gas is so bad that it was outlawed by international treaties signed by the United States in January of 1993. We said we would never use it against enemy troops again. Yet for six and one-half hours we subjected children, women, and old people to this chemical agent. What crime had they committed? They used it against these dangerous religious cultists.

Then the fire started after six and one-half hours. Anybody who has ever used CS gas knows that, pumped into an enclosed area, it is highly flammable. In fact, it's suspended in a powder called CAP, and it's like talcum powder. It is similar to what happens in a coal mine when a spark hits the fine dust. Or what can happen in a grain elevator from the fine dust. In Vietnam they pumped this gas into Viet Cong infiltration tunnels and lit a match, torching the whole tunnel.

The person they put in charge of the Waco investigation turned out to be an independent investigator who used to work for the ATF in Houston, Texas. His wife is the secretary of the head of the ATF office. So it wasn't really an independent investigation. Three weeks later they bulldozed the scene of the crime. So we'll never know what really happened in there.

This happened to these people because they were suspected of having illegal arms and because they were labeled a "dangerous religious cult." There are another 75-100 million people in this country who also have arms in the United States. What happens if the government suspects that Christians are a dangerous religious cult? Waco, Weaver, and Scott are precedents which, if the American people don't call someone to task on, could be repeated against you, your family, your church, Focus on the Family, or some other Christian ministries in this country.

A Powerful Centralized Government

There is always the possibility of a state of national emergency in this country which would involve martial law. The dictionary defines martial law as "a system of government under the direction of military authority." Basically, it's an arbitrary law proceeding directly from military power, having no constitutional or legislative sanction, and superseding all civil government. Martial law was imposed in Los Angeles during the riots in the spring of '92, and could have been declared nationally had the riots continued to spread during the summer.

The major elements of martial law are: 1) suspension of the writ of habeas corpus, 2) right to trial by jury, and 3) protection from illegal imprisonment. A state of national emergency could be used as a quantum leap toward a socialist America, lining up with the New World Order.

The president of the U.S. can issue executive orders during martial law. Hundreds of new executive orders (powers) have been passed by Congress over the past few decades, giving the president total dictatorial control over every aspect of American life during a state of emergency. Under a full state of emergency, anyone suspected of hate crimes; environmental, financial, or gun control crimes; or criminal violation of any of the tens of thousands of new government regulations can be imprisoned.

Government Surveillance of Citizens

Computers and other high-tech breakthroughs over the past few years have given the U.S. and other governments the ability to listen to, monitor, track, and keep citizens under surveillance, from the cradle to the grave. It was not available to Hitler in Nazi Germany. Or to the Communists in Russia, China, or the East bloc, until very recently.

Each adult American now has several dozen or more files in government computerized databases, usually keyed to your Social Security number. Dozens of different government agencies maintain millions of records on the American public. Articles about these records have been published in *Newsweek* and *Time*. Computerized profiles on each adult American were assembled by the IRS between 1985 and 1990, using tax, credit card, bank, medical, employment, police, passport, and other records drawn from various government databases, private credit bureaus, etc. Many phone calls, telexes, faxes, and certain U.S. mail are now regularly monitored by federal agencies.

Phones can now be made "hot on the hook," meaning even though your personal home telephone is hung up, someone may still be listening to you through it. The government has, and has used, the technology to go down to the local telephone switching station, connect to your private telephone number, and listen to conversations in your living room even though the phone is hung up. According to a 1992 report by the General Accounting Office entitled, "FBI Advance Communications Technologies Pose Wire-Tapping Challenges," it is the intent of the FBI to have the ability to tap every phone in America. The National Security Agency has monitored international phone calls to or from the U.S. for years. Computerized voice recognition on phones pick up key words from phone conversations which trigger the NSA tape recorders.

Several years ago, U.S. passports were made computer-readable. Now U.S., Canadian, Australian, German, and other European authorities are installing computers in airports. The computers will not only read passports, but also handprints, via infrared security readers. Data banks of computerized handprints will be developed over the next few years and linked to other government data bases so that an instant computer record for individuals will be flashed on a computer screen by waving a person's hand over a grocery store-type infrared scanner. This system is being set up and is being experimented with right now at the JFK airport in New York, in Europe, and in a few airports in Canada.

National I.D.

The government believes it is absolutely necessary for all Americans to have a national I.D. card. This new I.D. card will eventually be mandatory for all U.S. citizens. Most likely it will have biometric identification information, health care data, fingerprint and handprint data, and all tied to government databases. It has been designed to be a "smart card." A smart card is a tiny computer that looks like your credit card, but that can store 1,600 pages of data on you. And, of course you will be required to carry this card everywhere you go. Expect to see this pushed heavily in the media in the future.

Tracking Society

If the government wants to control people then they will move toward a cashless society, because privacy and cash make it much harder to control people. If the unwritten plan is to move toward a socialist America, or a New World Order, as in George Orwell's *1984*, they must be able to track, monitor, and control every aspect of a person's life.

Cash is trackless and difficult to trace, so it must be eliminated. Therefore, the goal should be to ultimately do away with currency and to force every American to use the computerized debit/credit system — where it is easily trackable. The liberals will simply argue that cash is the mother's milk of drug traffickers and money launderers, and therefore, if we want to stop drugs, we must make a small sacrifice and stop the use of cash. But if that sacrifice is our constitutional right to carry our own money, then I'm not sure that that's a small sacrifice.

Cars can now be tracked via small implanted computerized sending and receiving devices linked with government satellites. The U.S. government has spent heavily in money and research over the past 15 years to develop this system of people/vehicle tracking. In the near future, each new car will be required to have the computerized devices, or slots for the devices, installed at the factory.

Every square inch of the earth's surface can now be monitored by satellite; all persons and activities can now be watched. Lasers can be directed at a building from over a mile away and all conversations in that building can be listened to without the parties realizing it.

Money Laundering Laws

The first thing the Nazis did in 1930 to establish control over their people was to establish money crimes that were punishable by asset or property confiscation and imprisonment. A half-century later the same thing is happening here. The war on drugs and cash is the classic government power grab.

In the former Soviet Union, if the government wanted to apprehend and imprison someone who had committed no crime, they charged him with the catch-all crime of hooliganism. It was a generic charge. The American equivalent of hooliganism is the catch-all RICO, or conspiracy statutes. These were originally created to arrest and jail organized crime figures. In recent years, the government has used more and more frequently a new catch-all crime, punishable by imprisonment, confiscation of property, heavy fines, etc. It is called money laundering.

Most Americans suppose that money laundering refers primarily to the hidden, laundered movement of the cash profits from drug sales. And if that's what someone was doing, I would say, "Go get the dirty rats." But now it's being applied in broader areas: financial crime, broken financial regulations, the use of cash, avoidance of government cash reporting laws, unreported foreign bank accounts, unreported transfers of funds, or virtually anything a government bureaucrat wants it to mean. The definition is vague and seems to be ever-expanding.

IRS agents are greatly accelerating money laundering cases into situations where there's obviously no criminal intent, and certainly no involvement whatsoever with drugs or drug money. Remember, the IRS considers money laundering to be almost any effort you make to disguise your assets or to avoid completing a federal currency transaction or border-crossing form. The government's growing, expanding money laundering laws are becoming the basis for a total financial dictatorship in America, all under the guise of fighting the drug war. Please don't misunderstand, I am for fighting the drug war. But don't treat all Americans like we're guilty and then put controls on us to watch us in order to "fight the drug war."

The Treasury Department recently issued a booklet entitled *Money Laundering: A Banker's Guide to Avoiding Problems,* which contains a list of suspicious activities that the Treasury Department says fit the profile of a money launderer. Bank clerks are supposed to look for people who do these things and fill out a form about them if they do. 1) Paying off a delinquent loan all at once; 2) changing currency from small to large denominations; 3) buying cashier's checks, money orders, or traveler's checks, all now defined as cash, for less than $10,000. To me, it's not uncommon to take a trip to Europe and purchase two or three thousand dollars' worth of cashier's or traveler's checks. But, according to these guidelines, that's defined as a suspicious activity, and you should be reported. 4) Acting nervous while making large transactions with cash or monetary instruments. God help you if you just had a fight with your wife, if you've got the flu, if you're just really feeling bad, or whatever. If you act nervous, you could be reported. 5) Opening an account and using it as collateral for a loan; 6) presenting a transaction that involves a large number of $50 and $100 bills; 7) presenting a transaction without counting the cash first.

Murder, rape, and armed robbery now result in

smaller and less frequent jail terms or fines than the new federal crime of money laundering. In fact, the penalties for money laundering are 10 times more severe than the same crime prosecuted as tax evasion. You can receive, for the crime of money laundering, up to 10 years in jail, and a $250,000 fine.

Structuring Laws

Structuring is defined by the IRS as any effort to avoid reporting cash or other monetary transactions over $10,000, by breaking them down into smaller related transactions over any 12-month period. Monetary instruments included in structuring are cash, cashier's checks, money orders, and traveler's checks. Structuring falls under the category of money laundering and is a criminal offense punishable by up to 20 years in jail and up to a $500,000 fine. There's less penalty for robbing your local bank in broad daylight.

It's also against the law for a bank or merchant to tell you that you might be violating the law. This can get him prosecuted as part of your structuring conspiracy. If they think your behavior is suspicious, they must fill out a form on you without telling you and file it with the IRS, who will promptly audit you or begin a criminal investigation. The IRS admits that 85 percent of the people accused of structuring committed no other crime than seeking to protect their privacy. The courts have upheld numerous criminal structuring convictions for violations that concealed no criminal activity. If the government wins the conviction, the judge must sentence the criminal to a mandatory prison sentence. This gives the lie to the argument that the money laundering/structuring laws are enforced to get drug dealers and fight the war on drugs.

Money laundering and structuring laws have little to do with the war on drugs. But they can be used as the excuse, a legal loophole, for the liberal government bureaucrats to charge innocent people with violations. They're a way to move us toward a cash-less society, with Orwellian-type controls on the American people. Last year, 52,000 Americans had assets seized, totaling over $800 million. Houses, cars, buildings, businesses, real estate, brokerage accounts, airplanes, etc.

I don't think you should violate any tax laws or any money-laundering laws. But you do need to understand them or risk having your property seized by the government.

Now, I've painted a rather dim picture, and one could say these things do have some prophetic significance, and I think they really do. One could say we probably are plunging toward Armageddon and the second coming of Jesus Christ (and I hope I'm not considered to be a dangerous religious cultist for saying that), but we could be plunging toward Christ's return. Maybe it's 2 years, 5 years, 10 years, or 100 years away. I don't know.

But I know this: My God is still in control. He's in control of leaders, nations, history, and He's in control of our individual lives. I believe God is looking for people who, as it says in Ezekiel 22, will stand in the gap. People who will take a stand for Jesus Christ.

But taking a stand for Jesus Christ also comes with consequences. All over the world, more than at any time in church history, believers are being martyred for their belief in Jesus Christ. If you take a stand, you will be eventually singled out through data, surveillance, tax profiles, or through whatever the enemy may have available to use. Before this decade is out, many more born-again believers could be martyred for the cause of Jesus Christ. I believe we're moving towards eventual persecution of the Christian church and people who believe in traditional values, the Constitution, and who are called conservatives.

I'm not anti-government. I am a pro-Constitutionalist. In this country we have two documents which have governed this country for the first 220 or so years of our history: the Bible and the Constitution. We need to go back to trusting those or risk losing our great nation to the powers of darkness. Now, if that makes me politically incorrect, so be it.

I think there's a two-fold message in the Bible. I believe we are to take an active stand for Jesus Christ and to take an active stand against evil. I don't see enough Christians who seem to even recognize evil. But as long as they're willing to stand up and take a stand against that evil, I think that God will turn things around in this country. I think there are a lot of American Christians who are beginning to wake up. A remnant.

Isaiah wanted to be a watchman and tell the people how bad things were. And God says, "Fine, you're hired. But go out and tell the people how rotten they are and how I'm really going to judge their country. They probably won't listen, you may not even escape with your life." Why should he do it? God explained, "You don't understand. There's a remnant of people in this country who have not bent their knee to Baal, who have remained faithful to Me and the old ways" (see Rom. 11:4). And they're the people who I believe are going to be used by God in great and mighty ways.

And who are the remnant? I think the remnant, in this country, are born-again, evangelical Christians who believe in traditional values, who believe in the Constitution, and who, frankly, are getting just a tad miffed at the people who are coming along and destroying our way of life.

"How, then, shall we live?" We know, as David said in Psalm 11, "our foundations are crumbling." How then shall we live in this day? "God, how do You want me to serve You? How do You want me to live? What position, what role do You want me to stand? How can I stand in the gap for You in these days?"

These are the most exciting times in world history, and also in the history of the United States. I wouldn't live in any other time period. I've got four kids, I home-school three of them. One of them just went off to college, and let me tell you, it's a great time for them to grow up. Because a Christian who is motivated to serve God at any cost, who is sold out for our Lord Jesus Christ, can make such an incredible difference in this country in which we live.

4

The Armageddon Scenario

Hal Lindsey

As one who has studied prophecy for the last 38 years, I can honestly say that these are the days I've dreamed of ever since I became a Christian. Why? Prophetic events are accelerating. I used to get excited if I saw a significant event in prophecy occur every three or four years. Now you can hardly pick up a newspaper or look at a television newscast without seeing something that directly relates to the predicted scenario of events that would come together in concert just before the return of Christ.

I'm not a date setter because I don't know the day or the hour when Christ is coming back, but I know He commanded us to know the general time of His return and we are in it. We are drawing very near to the time when we'll hear the footsteps of Christ at the very threshold of heaven, ready to return for us. And so much has happened since I wrote *The Late, Great Planet Earth*[1] that I feel an update is in order.

Questions

The most interesting factors have come together in what Jesus said in Matthew 24. As Jesus was sitting on the Mount of Olives, His disciples came to Him privately, saying, "Tell us?" (Jesus had just told them that the temple would be destroyed and not one stone would be left upon the other.) The disciples ask three questions. "Tell us when will these things be?" In other words, "When is the temple going to be torn down?" Second, "What will be the sign of Your coming?" This meant coming in power as Messiah the King. And third, "What will be the sign of the end of the age?" Matthew chooses not to record Jesus' answer to the first question, but Luke does in Chapter 21:8-24. In those verses, Jesus describes what would happen in the interlude between the destruction of the temple in A.D. 70 and the return of Christ.

Matthew 24 records Jesus' answers to the second and third questions. He starts by telling the disciples the signs of His coming and those of the end of the age. Jesus says in verse 4, "See to it that no one misleads you. For many will come in my name, saying 'I am the messiah,' and will mislead many." The first sign is that of religious deception; impostors pretending to be messiahs and a departure from the truth of the Word of God. This is the first sign.

Certainly we have seen this developing, especially since the nineteenth century, and it has become full blown in the twentieth century to the point where we have people who claim to be Christ. The incident at Waco with the Branch Davidians is just one of the latest, but certainly not the last. There will be many of those, I believe.

"But that is not yet the end," Jesus says. Verse 8 is the key. When He finishes naming the signs He says, "But all of these things are merely the beginning of birth pangs." Men know theoretically; many women know it experientially, when you're about to have a baby, you begin to get severe pains in your abdomen and they get more frequent and more intense as you get closer to actually giving birth. This is the key to understanding the signs He gives.

The first birth pang is religious deception. According to 2 Thessalonians 2 there would be a great turning to satanic-type religions and the occult. There are also warnings of this in 2 Timothy 3, 1 Timothy 4, and in the Book of Jude, where it says that Christianity would retreat from believing the Word of God as the infallible Word, retreat from proclaiming the message of Christ, and the vacuum would be taken up by an unprecedented turning to the occult. I believe it's starting to accelerate. Everything is accelerating like birth pangs, becoming more frequent, more intense.

Then Jesus says, "You will be hearing of wars and rumors of wars [that's His way of saying "hot wars and cold wars"], but see to it that you are not alarmed. Such things must happen, but the end is still to come" (Matt. 24:6;NIV). In other words, there would be a period of constant warfare. A period where there would be not only actual war, but the constant threat of war. We've seen that.

The twentieth century will go down in history as the most destructive period of all human history as far as warfare is concerned. More people have been killed in wars in the twentieth century than in all of the other centuries put together. And now we have weapons that are aptly called weapons of mass destruction. Things that are predicted in the Bible can now be accomplished by the human race. Bible passages that were once thought to be supernatural interventions of God (and certainly this could still be the case) with a tremendous loss of life in the days just before Christ's return, these things are now technically possible and the weapons are already in the arsenals of many key countries predicted as being part of this last war. It is already in place.

We are not headed toward a world that's safer; we're not headed toward a world that is going to be at peace. We're headed into the exact scenario the prophets said: a time of overconfidence, a time of foolishness on the part of nations where there is greater danger than ever before.

The United States is probably in its gravest danger since the early days of independence. We were in great danger then — we're in worse shape now because we have very few watchmen on the wall who are alert to what's happening. As a result, we have a Congress that cut our armed forces, making it impossible for us to defend ourselves. At the same time, politicians tout us as the "policemen of the world." We do the dirty work and the credit goes to the United

Nations. We're over-extending what armed forces we have left, and now weapons existing in very unstable places are capable of destroying the entire human race. In Russia we have no idea what will happen next *week,* much less the next 20 years . . . and they still possess weapons of mass destruction.

Jesus also said, "Nation will rise against nation, and kingdom against kingdom. There will be famines and earthquakes in various places" (Matt. 24:7;NIV). Well, the next birth pang is one of international revolutions. "Kingdom rising against kingdom." We've certainly seen that. Communism has caused revolution to break out in so many places it's not even a question. But Jesus also says there will be famines.

Famine has been a fact of life since 1974. Since 1974, there has been a major, horrible famine in at least one place in the world *at all times.* Famine stems from many factors, but the population explosion certainly has been a major contributing factor. When I was born, there were two billion people in the world. It took the world from the beginning of man to 1850 to reach the first billion; from 1850 to 1930 to reach the second billion; from 1930 to 1960 to reach the third billion; from 1960 to 1975, the fourth billion; and from 1975 to 1985 to reach the fifth billion. This type of rapid geometric explosion has put tremendous stress on every social problem man has ever had. And now it's impossible to stamp out famine. In fact, famine will only increase because the population is greatest in the countries that can least afford it.

Why is all this important? It's important because it's as Jesus described. These pangs are not related. They affect the world, but they're not inter-dependent. I think this is important because Jesus pointed out easily recognized world conditions that would occur in concert. They're increasing in frequency and intensity so we would be sure to notice and say, "This is the time."

Jesus also says there would be earthquakes. The frequency of earthquakes in the last 30 years has roughly tripled each decade. Earthquakes in the 1990s have already tripled, and we are well on our way to being the record decade for large, killer earthquakes. Everyone seems to be aware of the fact that something unusual is happening. No one knows exactly why earthquakes of major magnitude have increased in such frequency in so many places. But they have — and at the precise time all these other factors are occurring.

Luke adds a final birth pang to this list. He records, in Luke 21:11, "And there will be great earthquakes, and in various places, plagues." He adds *plagues* to the scenario.

When I spoke about this birth pang 20 years ago, people would laugh — especially those in the medical profession — and they would say, "Because of miracle drugs and the many advances we've made in the field of medicine, the likelihood of a world plague is very remote."

Well, Jesus said there would be a plague like the other birth pangs, something of major magnitude, something unprecedented. Something that would spread. Well, we are now experiencing the ultimate plague of all time. I'm sure you've heard plenty about it. But it is the first plague in history that's politically protected. The insanity of our leaders, afraid of losing the homosexual vote, has put the whole nation at risk. People whose immune systems are compromised by the HIV virus have become walking petri dishes, incubating and spawning a host of new disease strains such as a mutant version of tuberculosis, which has a 60 percent fatality rate. If a person is diagnosed as having TB, he's quarantined. And yet the HIV+ person who created the mutant TB cannot even be *reported* as having HIV, much less quarantined — and it's 100 percent fatal. Where's the logic in that?

Jesus said there would be plagues, and the worst plague of all time is AIDS because it removes our immunity to everything. Most people who have AIDS die not from AIDS, but from pneumonia or an infection. AIDS wipes out their immune system, so they'll die from one of many causes. It's a plague to end all plagues; Jesus said it would come.

Jesus continues in Matthew 24:25, "And there will be signs in the sun and moon and stars, and upon the earth, dismay among nations in perplexity, at the roaring of the sea and the waves, men fainting from fear in the expectation of the things which are coming upon the world. For the power of the heavens will be shaken." He's talking about the power of the atmosphere as well as interstellar space. Jesus is describing another birth pang, one of tremendous changes in global weather patterns. I believe He's also talking about phenomena from space that would strike terror in the hearts of people.

It's interesting that astronomers today are concerned because they have spotted a meteor cluster that seems to be headed toward earth. Even if it hits the earth with a glancing blow, it will wipe out anywhere from a fourth to a third of the earth's population. And there is very little we can do about it because it's a cluster of meteorites. If we were to fire a thermonuclear weapon at it, it wouldn't stop it from coming; it would only spread so that instead of being a "rifle shot" at planet Earth, it would be more like a "shotgun shot." Astronomers are tracking it, and there's a growing alarm that it's headed toward our orbit.

This may be one of the things Jesus is warning about here, but He's definitely warning about global weather pattern changes because He talks about men in dismay, and there being "distress of nations, with perplexity; the sea and the waves roaring; Men's hearts failing them for fear, and for looking after those things which are coming on the earth: for the powers of heaven shall be shaken" (Luke 21:25-26;KJV). So something is going to affect the weather patterns of the planet so there will be storms of such magnitude people will be dropping like flies from sheer terror. Dropping dead of heart attacks from fear.

During the last five years we have clocked typhoons and hurricanes with the greatest velocity ever recorded, and they are still growing in intensity. Now, many people will tell you, "We've had freak weather before. There are times when one part of the world will have drought, and then it will have a flood, and so forth." Yeah, that's true. But this is the first time we've had freak weather in so many places at the same time. That's new. And I believe this is part of what Jesus was referring to when He said this will be a birth pang in concert with the other things, causing us to see that His return is very near.

Antichrist Is Alive

As I look at these things, it's unmistakable. I believe that Christ's coming must be very near because we see these things in an advanced state of fulfillment. But these are general signs. There are some technical realities hidden in prophecy that couldn't be possible until this present time. For instance, read Revelation 13:16-17 where it says, speaking of the dictator, (we call him the Antichrist) "He also forced everyone, small and great, rich and poor, free and slave, to receive a mark on his right hand or on his forehead, so that no one could buy or sell unless he had the mark, which is the name of the beast or the number of his name." In Revelation 13:7, it talks about the whole world being brought under the control of this person. Those in past generations who looked at this must have wondered, "How could one man cause every person — man, woman, and child — on the face of this planet to be numbered and then be able to keep track of them?" It was impossible in other generations, but now, just at the time when all of the other predicted events are happening, we have the technical ability for this Antichrist to come in and number every person on earth and have instant access to those that have violated it. We're talking about a total control of the world through economics . . . and it's child's play.

With today's technology it is now easy for computers to not only identify every person on earth, but to also keep a dossier, a history, on every person. Technically, a chip can be placed under the skin of the forehead or the forehand, and it will have much more than a number.

I believe the 666 is a prefix. Everyone will have the same prefix on his number, but each one will have an individual number that follows. And I think we're being set up right now. Numbers are being simplified and unified right now. The one basic number (and when it was given, it was promised never to be used for this) is your Social Security number. Your Social Security number is the most basic identification you have.

When the Antichrist comes on the scene (and he's already alive somewhere in Europe; I'm sure of it), you will have to swear allegiance to him as the supreme ruler and deity in order to buy, sell, or hold a job. When you do that, the prefix will be added to your number. It will probably not be a tattoo; I think people will have a chip put under the skin of their hand or their forehead. I can see it all now . . . you're not really chic, you're really not in vogue, unless you have this beauty spot where the chip was implanted.

Special computers, when you get within 10 feet, will monitor you and will immediately pick up your number and everything about you. This is possible right now. Technically this prophecy can be fulfilled today. But there's more!

Days Cut Short

Look at Matthew 24 again for a moment. Jesus makes a very important statement in verses 21-22. He said, "For then there will be a great Tribulation." He's talking about the events that occur just before His return in the final seven years that immediately precede His return. He says, "For then there will be a great Tribulation such as has not occurred since the beginning of the world until now, nor ever shall. And unless those days had been cut short, no life would have been saved. But for the sake of the elect, those days shall be cut short." Jesus said that there would come a time just immediately before He returns when life on this planet would be in jeopardy of being extinguished.

Once again, when in history could that have happened? Never in history has mankind developed a weapon that he didn't ultimately use, and I believe man will also use *these* weapons of mass destruction, especially thermonuclear, biological, and chemical weapons. I believe there's evidence in the Scripture of that. Look at Isaiah 13.

Isaiah lived 2,700 years ago, and he says in Isaiah 13:12 (speaking of the events that will end man's dominance of the world), "I will make mortal man scarcer than the pure gold, and mankind than the gold of Ophir." Isaiah is speaking about a time in which the loss of life is so great God says mankind will be scarcer than the gold of Ophir. And that's pretty scarce (we've never found the gold supply that was part of the Garden of Eden). We're talking about a tremendous loss of life.

Now read Isaiah 24:1-6. Many people ask me how they can tell when a passage applies to the events that lead to the coming of the Messiah. Many times the passages are couched in prophecies that were warning kingdoms in Isaiah's day. I have found that the prophecies will increase in magnitude and scope to include a judgment on the whole world, which is climaxed by the Messiah's coming and setting up His kingdom. So these passages are often couched in prophecies that start out about current events and then will increase in scope to include events of the final days. Here is one example:

> Behold the Lord lays the earth waste, devastates it, distorts its surface and scatters its inhabitants. The people will be like the priest, the servant like his master, the maid like her mistress, the buyer like the seller, the lender like the borrower, and the creditor like the debtor. The earth will be completely laid waste and completely despoiled. The Lord has spoken His word. The earth mourns and withers, the world fades and withers, the exalted of the people of the earth fade away. The earth is also polluted by its inhabitants (Isa. 24:1-5).

I think we've pretty well fulfilled that already. The earth has been polluted by its inhabitants, and

Isaiah tells us why: "They have transgressed the laws, changed the ordinance, broken the everlasting covenant" (Isa. 24:5;KJV). Specifically, God set the laws of nature in motion when He created and restored this planet. We've broken those laws, and we're reaping a whirlwind because of the way we have polluted and distorted and destroyed the ecology of this planet. So in verse 6 it says, "Therefore, a curse devours the earth. Those who live in it are held guilty. Therefore, the inhabitants of the earth are burned and few men are left."

Now turn to the Book of Revelation: "I looked, and when he broke the sixth seal, there was a great earthquake." It doesn't mean earthquake, necessarily. The word simply means "a violent shaking." In other words, there was a violent shaking of the earth.

> The sun became black as sackcloth made of hair. The whole moon became like blood. The stars of the sky (literally, a meteor) fell to the earth as a fig tree casts its unripe figs when shaken by a great wind. The sky was split apart like a scroll when it is rolled up and every mountain and island were moved out of their place. The kings of the earth and the great men and commanders and the rich and the strong and every slave and free man hid themselves in the caves and among the rocks of the mountains. And they said to the mountains and to the rocks, "Fall on us, and hide us

from the presence of him who sits on
the throne" (Rev. 6:12-16;NIV).

This is a tremendous judgment. And the previ-
ous verses describe judgments where a fourth of the
population of the earth would die from war, famine,
plague, and the wild beasts of the earth. And then it
opens up the seal, and there is this tremendous shaking.

The Holy Spirit revealed to me that the key to
understanding these passages is to realize that John, a
first century man, was put in a divine time machine
and shot up to what will probably be somewhere
around the end of the twentieth century. We're not
there yet; he's already been there. He was catapulted
by the miracle of the Holy Spirit to actually see and
hear what he writes about here, what's going to
happen. Then he was brought back to the first century,
and was told to write about it. And here's the key: How
could a first century man write about things of a
highly scientific and technical age far beyond his
experience? The only way would be to write and say
it looked like or it was like phenomena with which he
was familiar.

Now, he had seen a shooting star, he had seen
a meteor, he had seen or heard of earthquakes, he
knew about how they could shake the land, and using
his first century experience, he tried to write what he
had seen. He tried to describe it. I believe when you
look at this passage in that light, you have a very, very
accurate picture of a tremendous nuclear holocaust —
and this is only Phase One. There's another one.

When he talks about meteors coming from the sky like ripe figs in verse 13, I believe he's describing that which are now in silos, and hidden in caves and railroad tunnels all over the old Soviet Union — intercontinental ballistic missiles with multiple warheads. When these are fired at a target, they go up out of the earth's atmosphere, make an arc, and then separate and travel to different targets. When they re-enter the earth's atmosphere, they look like meteors, or shooting stars. I believe that's what John saw, and he was describing it. When he talks about the atmosphere being rolled up like a scroll, he's describing one of the destructive parts of an atomic explosion; the tremendous explosion pushes back the atmosphere. It literally pushes it back on itself. It rolls it up like a scroll. I believe John gave us a pretty accurate description of this. He also talks about the sun becoming black like sackcloth. Have you ever heard of the nuclear winter that's predicted if we have an all-out nuclear war? The debris would be so tremendous in the atmosphere that it would blot out the sun. I've been in Los Angeles on days of great pollution, and the moon turns red because you're looking at it through pollution. I believe this is what John is describing.

Now turn to Revelation 8. It describes the next series of judgments, which are more severe. Whereas a fourth of the earth's population was destroyed in the first series, in chapter 9 a third of those who remain will be killed. Together, over half the present population of the earth will be killed. We have over 5 billion people on this planet right now. If this judgment was to occur now, more than two and one–half billion people would be killed. We discover how it's going to happen in Revelation 8:7: "The first angel sounded and there came hail and fire mixed with blood. And they were thrown to the earth, and a third of the earth was burned up. A third of the trees were burned up. And all the green grass was burned up."

It talks about a hail of fire mixed with blood. I believe John's describing a tremendous fire storm that starts when you have several nuclear blasts in close proximity. It will burn up a third of the trees. Think of the enormity of this. We're concerned about the destruction of the rain forests in Brazil, and it is terrible, but nothing compared to a third of the trees on earth burning up and all green grass burned. This includes wheat and things of that nature also.

And then the second angel sounds in verse 8. "And something like. . . ." Notice John is clear here. He says, "something like." In other words, he didn't know what it was, but he described what it "looked like" to him. "Something like a great mountain burning with fire was thrown into the sea, and a third of the sea became blood, a third of the creatures which were in the sea and had life died. And a third of the ships were destroyed."

We're talking about something of such enormity here, it's hard to imagine. But we have weapons right now that can do this. We've known for some time that Russia, even in this tremendous debacle of domestic economics, is still building Red October-class nuclear submarines. We know that there are some 32 of them operating right now. Each one has 200 thermonuclear warheads on board. We have not only submarines, but aircraft carriers, cruisers, and so forth, with all kinds of nuclear weapons on them. France has this kind of weaponry, too, and now some of the most unstable nations in the world are getting nuclear capabilities, also. So it's not beyond our imagination now for this sort of thing to take place, and the Bible says it will take place shortly before the return of Jesus Christ. When John says it looks like a great mountain, burning with fires, thrown into the sea, I believe it's describing a nuclear naval battle that will destroy a third of the ocean as well as a third of all the ships in the world . . . and we have never had such capability until now.

I believe these sorts of things are very, very near. But what is the scenario that will touch it all off? The key has always been the rebirth of the state of Israel and the city of Jerusalem being under Israeli control.

Smoldering Hatred

The Bible talks about an ancient hatred that has existed for 4,000 years between the descendants of Ishmael and the descendants of Isaac and Jacob: the Arab and the Jew. When Israel was reborn in 1948, and then when it recaptured and kept Old Jerusalem in 1967, the stage was set for an eventual war and the political powers are developing right before our eyes. It's extremely interesting that the hatred the Arabs have had for thousands of years for the Israelites has now been exported by the religion of Islam.

The writings of Mohammed, known as the Koran, says the Jew is to be under perpetual persecution, that they're not worthy to live in the same land with the Muslims, and that they are to be kept in subjection, which is their just reward. There are now 1.2 billion Muslims in the world today, and they are not just the Arabs. People who are not Arab at all become part of a religion based on the culture of seventh-century Arabia. To be a good Muslim, you have to adopt that culture, which includes a hatred for the Jew. The Muslim problem with the state of Israel is not how big it is, it is its very existence. They can never give up enough land to be acceptable. If they had a state of Israel on 400 square meters, it still wouldn't be acceptable, because it's on what the Muslims call "His Holy Land." Not just Jerusalem, but all of what is called Israel today.

Jerusalem is the third holiest place of the Islamic faith. Zechariah 12:2-3 says that a smoldering hatred will explode into a flame, setting off the last war of the world. Zechariah 12, 13, and 14 describe the battle over Jerusalem from the standpoint of Israel. But Zechariah 12 also says that all the nations of the world are going to be burdened over a conflict concerning Jerusalem; all the nations of the world will go to war because of Jerusalem. The stage is set.

The prophets said there would be four basic spheres of political power in place when Israel was reborn as a nation in the last days. The first sphere would be the Muslim nations, which would band together because of their mutual hatred of Israel. They're called "the kings of the south" in Daniel 11:

40-45 (which, incidentally, is an exact battle plan of how the last war of the world will develop).

The next sphere of power is a group headed by what the Bible calls the people from the uttermost north, the descendants of Magog. I believe that it can be proven conclusively that the descendants of Magog are the modern ethnic Russians. So the falling apart of the Soviet Union had nothing to do with the fulfillment of this prophecy except that it put this in a better perspective of what Ezekiel predicted. Ezekiel never predicted that the Russians would be world conquerors, but a very powerful regional power that would join in with the Arabs in a war against Israel. *Intelligence Digest* reported in the August 1993 issue: "Since the breakup of the Soviet Union, this service has consistently argued that Russia will eventually return to its traditional role of heading up an anti–western, predominately Islamic third–world alliance. We now can say that is confirmed."

For two years, I've been following *Intelligence Digest's* intelligence work showing that the Russian republic has signed agreements with Iran and Syria. Russia cannot compete economically in the industrialized world, so they've gone to the Third World where they *can* dominate. But to do this they have to make peace with the Muslims, because the Muslims are the majority in the Third World. Another reason for these agreements is that Russia greatly fears the trouble that Islamic fundamentalism can cause in the six former Soviet Union republics that are Muslim, and also with the Muslim population that exists in Russia itself. Part of the agreements state that in the event of a major war in the Middle East, Russia will fight alongside the Muslims. This covenant has already been signed by Yeltsin; Ezekiel 38 is now guaranteed. It's already in place. These two powers will launch the first attack, and it will be because of the Islamic doctrine that whenever a holy place of the Islamic faith is taken, it's a matter of Allah's honor to get it back, no matter what the cost. Jihad, that's what we're going to have. There can be no peace as long as Islam does not have Jerusalem.

And let me tell you something — the Jews are not going to give it back because there can be no Judaism without Jerusalem. You might as well give up the soul of Israel, I was told, if you give up Jerusalem. One of their leading politicians once told me, "Hey, we've been praying toward Jerusalem from every part of this globe, from every nation, for 2,000 years. And maybe we could've prayed another 1,000 years to get it. But now that we have it, there's no power in hell that'll take it from us." The issue that's going to cause Armageddon is already locked into place. The two spheres of power that are going to invade and start Armageddon are already bound together by treaty. Does it have to be any more clear that Jesus is on the brink of coming back?

China Another Key

But there's another sphere of power. Revelation 16:12–16 speaks of the kings of the East being mustered to come into the Middle East once war has broken out there. In Revelation 9 it talks about this same power coming from the east of the Euphrates

River. Now the Euphrates River was important in the time of John, because in those days everything east of the Euphrates was called Asia. So when it speaks of this army of 200 million coming from the east of the Euphrates (and it's done by demonic activity stirring it up), it means that the kings of the east, plural, are going to come from Asia and, for the first time, come en masse into the Middle East. It's never happened in history, but it's going to.

I just studied a report, a very elaborate report, about the rise of Asia. It says, "Beijing has mapped out a course to become the world's biggest economy by the year 2025. The chances are they will achieve their objective ahead of schedule, probably by the year 2010." (I hate to disappoint them; I don't think they're going to make it. I don't think they'll have that much time.) "What Japan's industrious are looking for is a marriage of convenience between China's labor and raw materials and Japan's capital and technology. Now Japanese investment in China is booming." They say China is going to become the leading economic giant of the world by the year 2025, perhaps as early as the year 2010. This report shows that the Chinese have had a 100-year program planned, 100 years from 1949 when they became a Communist nation. Their 100-year plan has been to first consolidate all the people, wipe out the warlords, retrain them from the worship of the ancestors to a godless, atheistic, Communist point of view, and then develop them by using capitalism in certain, selected places, to develop them economically so they can then build a military that's commensurate with a world–class economy. They are now well on their way toward achieving that ahead of their 100-year goal.

I believe China is moving rapidly in this role predicted by the prophets. They are not making the same mistake Russia did. The report reveals that the leaders of China, with this long-range plan, have always planned to keep the leadership of the nation politically Communist, to make certain steps backwards in the dialectical materialism philosophy, certain steps backwards where they'll use capitalism just long enough to build up the economy to become a world power. You can go into any store now, and you'll find most of the articles of clothing were made in China. This is enabling them to use capitalism to achieve their end of ultimate global domination. That's what they want, and they don't want to make the same mistake of building their military too fast because they know you have to have a domestic economy that can support a massive military. This is where Russia and the Soviet Union made their mistake. We know they just did a tremendous revamping of their whole military. They've consolidated seven separate military districts and centralized them so that they're all under the command of the central committee, the Communist party. China saw how quickly the army of the Soviet Union fell apart once the political side of the Soviet Union fell apart. They don't want to make that same mistake. China has even signed a treaty with India, linking their mutual defense together. Do you know what this has done? China alone has one-fourth of the world's population. But when you link them together with India (and also with Japan) this coalition encompasses 42 percent of the world's population. Kings, plural, of the east. I believe these are the ones that are going to come.

India now has a population of 800 million; China has a population of 1.2 billion. So you've got 2 billion people there alone. They are the third sphere of political power. They're in place right now. Revelation 9 tells us this army of 200 million will wipe out one-third of the population of the earth with fire and brimstone. I believe that's referring to nuclear weapons again.

All Together Now

The last sphere of political power is rapidly coming into place, also. You've heard a lot about the New World Order, the coming world government. These spheres of power will, for a short while, be brought together into a one-world government. It will take the charismatic leadership of the Antichrist to do that. I don't believe we will have a world government before the Antichrist comes, but I believe we'll be set up for it. I think we have the model for it being developed right now. The EEC openly says they are developing a model for a world federal government. That's their goal. I believe we'll have many attempts at a world government, I believe we'll have it all set up, but it takes a leader of unprecedented talent to bring together a world government when you've got over five billion people in the world, and when you've got religions of all kinds dividing people, racial hatreds dividing people, and national rivalries that have existed for centuries. How are you going to hold those people together? Only by a man who is possessed by Satan himself, the Antichrist. Satan is going to give him all of his power and authority, the Bible says.

One man with all the power of Lucifer? Lucifer is the most powerful being God ever created, so when it says all that power will be vested in one man, look out. This man is alive somewhere in the world today. And I believe he's just waiting for that time, the cue, when God will allow Satan to reveal him. Why can't he be revealed right now? It's very clear in 2 Thessalonians 2. Because we're still here! That's why.

No one can get too giddy and happy about the things I've been writing about. But now let me give you some good news. We're not going to be here when all this is going on! When it says in 2 Thessalonians 2:7 that "the one who now holds it back will continue to do so till he is taken out of the way. And then it the lawless one will be revealed," it's talking about a special restraining ministry of the Holy Spirit. And what is He restraining? The mystery of lawlessness. That mysterious part of the world system that captivates the mind of all men, even Christians who are not walking in the Spirit, and leads them into lawlessness away from God. The Holy Spirit is the only One who could restrain it from the time of Paul right up until the time the Antichrist is revealed. He's been doing this in a special way, in order to keep the promise that Jesus made when He first announced the coming of the Church.

When did Jesus first announce the coming of

the Church? The first mention of a church was in Matthew 16 when he asked Peter and the disciples, "Whom do men say that I am?" Peter stood up and said the one brilliant thing he did in all the Gospels. Peter said, "Thou art the Messiah, the Son of the Living God." And Jesus said, "Blessed are you Simon, son of John, for flesh and blood didn't show it to you; My Father did. Upon this rock I will build my Church and the gates of Hell shall not prevail against it." That is the promise.

The profession of faith that Peter had just made is the rock upon which Jesus would build His church. We know that because rock is *petra* in the Greek, and Peter's name is *petros*. *Petros* is masculine; *petra* is neuter. The modifier and the object it modifies have to be the same gender, so He's not saying Peter was the rock on which the Church would be built; He is referring back to the profession of faith Peter had just made. And He said, "The gates of hell will not prevail against the Church."

Now, if the Holy Spirit, since the day of Pentecost when the Church was born, was *not* restraining Satan and all the mystery of lawlessness, the Church would have been destroyed a long time ago. What is predicted in 2 Thessalonians 2:6-8 is a reversal of Pentecost. At Pentecost, the Holy Spirit came and took permanent, personal residence in every believer who corporately represents the body of Christ, which is the one true Church. He has been restraining through His personal presence in the Church on the earth. You can't take Him out of the world personally unless you take the containers in which He dwells out with Him. You can't take the Holy Spirit out of the world without taking the Church with Him, because He's been personally present in the Church since its birth on the day of Pentecost. So when the Bible says the restrainer is taken out of the way, it means that the Church is gone, and immediately Satan will unveil his masterpiece, the Antichrist, and he's going to do it with a spectacular occultic act.

This person is going to receive a mortal wound from which he will be miraculously raised up by Satan. This will catch the whole world's attention. Revelation 13:1-4 says the whole world is going to marvel because of that miracle, and that's why they immediately give him such attention and such immediate acceptance. I believe there'll be some other things, perhaps a demonic, fake landing of an extraterrestrial spaceship with extraterrestrials coming and saying, "We've come back! We planted you on this earth, and we've now come back to enforce what we started and to lead you to your next quantum leap in understanding." Something like that seems to be implied, because the Bible says God is going to send a delusion that will cause the whole world to believe the lie. How else could you get Muslims, Jews, Presbyterians, Episcopalians, Baptists, and all of those to band together into one religion and go into a one-world government? The whole psyche is going to have to be reset for people to go together into one religion. I believe God's got it all planned. I believe it's all set up, and I believe we're on the very threshold of Christ's return.

At the Door

I always come back to the parable of the fig tree, because Jesus said, "Learn it." After He gave the many signs that would precede His coming He said, "Now learn the sign of the fig tree. When its limbs first become tender and it puts forth leaves, you know that summer is near." This parable has one basic point: How to know the general time that summer is near. Then Jesus applies it. He says, "Even so, when you see all these things," and "all these things" referred back to the prophecies He had just given, and the prophecies that talk about the things that would precede His coming. He says, "When you see all of these, recognize I'm at the door. Truly, I say to you, this generation will not pass away until all is fulfilled." (Matt. 24:32-34).

We are that generation without a shadow of a doubt. The leaves on the fig tree were symbolic of the events of prophecy that I've just described to you. For us who are saved, this is wonderful news. But for those who are not, I have but one warning: 2 Thessalonians 2 says that everyone who hears the gospel, understands it, and rejects it, God will blind and never give a second chance. Now there will be millions who will believe during the Tribulation because they may have heard the gospel but they didn't understand it.

I'm about to tell you what it means, so you won't have any excuse. When Jesus came the first time He became a man and lived a sinless life in order to qualify to take the rap for your sins and mine. He qualified because He had no sin of His own, to die in your place and in my place, for every time we break God's law in thought, word, or deed. Right now, I challenge you: God doesn't care how bad you've been (Rom. 3:23). He's not impressed with how good you've been.

No matter what state you're in, if you will, right now, receive the gift of pardon that Jesus Christ died to give you. He'll give you eternal life, and He'll put you in His eternal family.

And on that day, which I believe is soon, when Christ comes for His own, you will be caught up with us, instantaneously, to meet Christ in the air, changed from mortal to immortal without seeing physical death. This is what Jesus promises He's going to do.

5

Europe: The Stage Is Set for World Dominance

Chuck Missler

I've spent the last 30 years in international corporate development, primarily with high-technology companies in the U.S. and in Europe, and some in Asia. I've made my living in corporate development, strategic planning. I've served on 12 public boards. I've been chairman of six of those; four of those were defense contractors. I mention that because I bring to this discussion perhaps a little different perspective than many of the people you have heard in the past.

Oriental Explosion

It's interesting as we explore the United States'

predicament, we seem to be in pretty bad shape. Most of us probably do not appreciate just how seriously we have deteriorated in terms of our productivity. In 1948, the United States produced 44 percent of the world's industrial output. We were eight times larger than Japan. Now we have a productivity growth that's the lowest in the industrial world. We have the highest trade deficit in history. In a recent reporting period, I was startled to notice two things. First of all, we posted a $12 billion trade deficit. Don't get confused; we've been talking so far primarily about our federal debt and our federal deficit. One of the things that concerns me as a practicing business executive is our ability to compete industrially, and the fact that we have billion dollar deficits is startling. But what bothers me more, the *New York Times* and other "experts" are also startled at just one month's trade deficit. We have the lowest rate of capital investment that we've ever had, one-third of Japan's.

Most of us may be startled to discover that the wealth of Japan surpassed the collective wealth of the United States in 1987. They've been growing, they've been working hard. There's one precinct in Tokyo that is worth more than all of Canada. The wealth of Japan today is more than twice the collective wealth of the United States. That may come as a shock to you. Why? Well, they're better educated, harder working, more efficient, and less violent than we are. They have three times the United States' productivity. It's interesting — many of you who have been following this may realize that recently they had a major drop, a major break in the Japanese stock market. They dropped almost 50 percent, about $10 trillion. That doesn't mean much to you and me as a number, but let me say that exceeds the collective value of all the stock exchanges on the planet Earth: All 83 of them. And yet, they absorbed that major loss.

One of the things that all the intelligence agencies are watching closely is the shifting of Japanese capital from the United States. First of all, they're removing it from the United States. Many of us who have been watching the news in the last number of years have noticed that the Japanese have invested heavily in all kinds of projects, all kinds of large buildings, a lot of fancy places throughout our country. They've bought major corporations, and so on. What everyone is beginning to notice is that they're quietly but very clearly withdrawing their capital from this country. And when you look carefully, you can begin to understand some of the reasons why. They are shifting that capital into a surprising area. They're shifting that capital into China. Now, if you know the history of the Orient, that may surprise you, because they're traditional enemies in many ways. But interestingly enough, both the Chinese and the Japanese cultures are very pragmatic. They know how to win. It's interesting to contemplate the ramifications of that shift. If you combine the capital and the technology of Japan with the labor and the raw materials of China, many experts are predicting that that may spark the biggest economic boom that the earth has ever seen. Now, I mention that really in passing, because I don't plan to dwell a lot on it, other than as one of the things that you want to be sensitive to as you develop your perspective (and I think the most valuable thing that you can have in business is perspective). The details you can always purchase. Once you know the questions to ask, the answers are forthcoming. The tough part, the valuable part, is putting things in perspective. And that's one of the main goals I think we all collectively have in putting together in *Steeling the Mind of America* is to develop an informed perspective.

Japan and China — keep an eye on them. China's going through a hard time and they've got a lot of problems. But it's the fundamental trends that are the things you need to be sensitive to and the rise of Asia is one of the things that we should keep an eye on. Those of you who are students of your Bible are probably aware there isn't a lot in the Scriptures about the Far East. But one of the things that will catch your eye; if it hasn't yet, is when you turn to Revelation 16:12. You know that, first of all, the Battle of Armageddon is a four-party conflict. The kings of the South trigger it off, the kings of the North come down, and then there's enormous power from one western confederacy. And about the time things are getting close to the climax, it says the ways of the kings of the East will be prepared. We find that there's a major force, a fourth force, coming from the Far East. The term in your English Bible is "the kings of the East," but it might be interesting to take note of the fact that that's not what the Greek says. The Greek says it's "the kings of the Rising Sun." Now, don't make too much of that because that is the classic linguistic way of speaking of the East. And yet, as most of you know, I have a rather bizarre view about the Scripture. I believe that every detail is there by design, and the Holy Spirit does deal in puns. So I find it fascinating that Japan and China are beginning to recognize a common destiny. I think that's kind of provocative.

The Dream

If God has the technology to create us in the first place, He has the technology to get a message to us. The question is, how does He authenticate it? One way he can authenticate it is to demonstrate that it came from outside the time domain and He does that by describing the end from the beginning. We call that prophecy.

Bear in mind I'm an engineer. I'm a technical nut. I was a radio ham when I was nine; I flew a light plane when I was a teenager. When other guys were hopping up cars in high school, I was building a digital computer in my garage. I ended up going to the Naval Academy and was in the air force. I took these specialty interests into the information sciences. And the great discovery in my life was the Bible. The discovery that every number, every place name, every detail of the original text is there by supernatural engineering, and it demonstrates its origin from being outside the time domain by writing history before it happens. It's in that spirit then, that I'd like to explore just briefly some passages that are probably very familiar to you and yet which have a profound impact on understanding what's going on today.

The Bible in general describes history through the lens of Israel. Generally, the Bible talks about things that happen on the Planet Earth as they impact

His chosen people, Israel. But there are several notable exceptions. There are two chapters in the Bible that specifically lay out all of Gentile history in advance. And they're found in the Book of Daniel. There are two chapters that you will want to study carefully in your next opportunity of casual time: Daniel 2 and Daniel 7. Daniel 2 takes place approximately six centuries before Christ was born. There's a guy by the name of Nabapolassar that was the king of the city/state called Babylon. The Assyrian Empire was on the decline. He had a very bright son by the name of Nebuchadnezzar who was his general. This shrewd technician was able to defeat a number of armies, and finally, he defeated Pharaoh Necho at the Battle of Carchemish, establishing Babylon as the world empire. And on his way home, he laid siege to Jerusalem. During the siege, he found out his dad had died. He was now king of Babylon. He succeeded in the siege, put in a vassal king, and went home to take over the throne.

Here's a young king who inherited the old palace guard. In that first siege, he took captives, set up a vassal king, took some hostages, Daniel and some of his friends, and they were deported as teenagers. The intent was to train them at graduate school and have them serve at the Babylonian court. Then this new king has a dream that really bothers him. He knows it's significant, but he also uses the opportunity to find out whether his staff can cut the mustard. He calls the men and tells them that he wants them to interpret the dream. He wants them to tell him what the dream was as well as the interpretation. Of course, they can't do it, and they're pretty shaken by that.

Nebuchadnezzar then explains his professional development program a little more clearly as he invokes his seizure laws. He sends the order out that all the people who are in that staff category are to be killed. He knew how to have the lay-offs when needed. He knew how to reduce head-count. So it turned out, Daniel's in that job description, but he, of course, petitions the king. He and his buddies have a prayer meeting, receive a message from God's angel, and Daniel not only tells the king what the dream was, but he also interprets it. All of this is detailed in Daniel 2.

The dream that Nebuchadnezzar had turns out to be not only a very dramatic story, but it also turns out that that dream lays out for you and me the history of mankind from that day to the end when God intervenes and has set up His own kingdom. The idiom that God used in the dream was a man, presumably a warrior with his arms folded, standing before them, a statue out of a series of metals. The head was of gold, the arms and chest of silver, belly and thighs of bronze, legs of iron. The feet are iron, but mixed with clay. Strange dream. The metals happen to be in the order of their specific gravity and also in decreasing value. Before you attempt to tackle chapter 2, I would read Daniel 7. Daniel 2 occurs when Daniel was a teenager just deported, early in his career. Daniel 7 happens when he's an older man. He's by a river at night, and God gives Daniel a series of visions of four beasts. The four beasts in Daniel 7 parallel, surprisingly, the details of Daniel 2. It's the two together that both play out the same materials, using a slightly different set of idioms.

The key point that I'd like to highlight is that there were four empires detailed. Now, the fourth empire goes through two phases. The first empire represented by the head of gold, of course, was Babylon, Nebuchadnezzar's empire, and that's interpreted for us right in the text. But that empire was to be succeeded by another: the Persians. They were to be succeeded by yet another, the Greeks. And the Greeks were to be succeeded by another, Rome. It's a good idea to look this up in your Bible in Daniel 2. We'll pick it up where Daniel's describing the dream. "This is the dream and we will tell its interpretation before the king. Thou, O king, are the king of kings, for the God of heaven has given thee a kingdom in power and strength and glory, and wherever the children of men dwell, the beasts of the field and the fowls of the heavens hath he given into thine hands and hath made thee ruler over them all. Thou art the head of gold" (Dan. 2:36-37). So Nebuchadnezzar was the first world empire on God's list of four. But verse 39 says, "And after thee shall arise another kingdom inferior to thee. And another third kingdom of bronze, which shall bear rule over all the earth." So he passes over those two kingdoms at this point, lightly. Then we focus on the fourth. And it's interesting that Daniel and the Holy Spirit detail for us a great deal about his fourth empire, which we know is the Roman Empire. Verse 40: "The four kingdoms shall be strong as iron, forasmuch iron breaketh in pieces and subdueth all things, and as iron that breaketh all these, shall it break in pieces and bruise."

It's interesting that you and I take for granted that these great empires, as one rose after the other, destroyed the one prior. That's not true. When Cyrus the Persian conquered Babylon, he did not destroy Babylon, he exploited it. He didn't interrupt their temple services. He attempted to be eclectic and take the best of the cultures. He might destroy the army, of course, in the battle, but it's interesting when Cyrus the Persian conquered Babylon, he did it without a battle; he did it by subterfuge. He went down the Euphrates, slipped his army under the gates when the water levels went down, and took it over. When you go to a London museum and look at the still of Cyrus, he brags to the world that he conquered Babylon without a battle. And he took advantage of it. In fact, Babylon was his secondary capitol. It was not destroyed at that time.

When Alexander the Great conquered the Persian Empire, he destroyed the army. It was a vendetta thing, but also, he didn't destroy what he conquered; he exploited it. His dream was to unite the world under a common world empire.

It was Rome who had the distinctive style that when they conquered a people, they took pride in what they could destroy. They burned the temple, they crushed the town, and so forth. It's interesting, in verse 40, that this fourth empire, "As iron breaketh in pieces, subdueth all things. And as iron breaketh all these, it shall break in pieces and bruise." Now, in verse 41, something subtle happens. We discover that this empire had two phases. And Daniel goes to some detail. Verse 41: "Whereas thou sawest the feet and the toes art of potter's clay and part of iron, the kingdom shall be divided, and there shall be in it the strength of iron, forasmuch as thou sawest the iron mixed with the clay, and as the toes of the feet were part iron and part clay, so the kingdom shall be partly strong and partly broken. And whereas thou sawest the iron mixed with clay, they shall mingle themselves with the seed of men, and they shall not adhere one to another, even as iron does not mix with clay." If we go to Daniel 7, we'll discover the same thing. These four empires are described in Daniel 7 as groups of strange beasts. But, again, it's Babylon, Persia, Greece, and then Rome. But Rome has two phases. Now it's interesting that in Daniel 2, we have this metallic image with the legs of iron, but the feet are iron mixed with clay.

Let's take a look at history, what really happened in 606 B.C. We talked about Babylon and Nebuchadnezzar, and so forth. It was 539 B.C. and Ugbaru conquered Babylon for Cyrus, establishing the Persian Empire. It was about 332 B.C., roughly two centuries later, when Alexander, this young man, in the Battle of Marathon, conquered the Persian Empire. It was about 68 B.C. on the banks of the Tiber, when Rome rose. Rome emerged as the largest and most ruthless of the empires under Julius Caesar. In 44 B.C., Julius Caesar was assassinated, and on it goes. It's interesting that in A.D. 284, Diocletianius divided the empire in two. That's interesting. Two legs, maybe. In A.D. 312 Constantine set up his empire and converted the Roman Empire to Christianity and transferred the capitol to Byzantium.

As we look at world history, it's interesting how it is parallel to visions of Daniel 2. There was Babylon. Who conquered the Babylonians? The Persians. Who conquered the Persians? The Greeks. Who conquered the Greeks? The Romans. Here's the question of the day: Who conquered the Romans? Nobody. About 476, that empire broke into pieces. It was divided, like Daniel talked about. Each of the pieces has had a bid at world dominion. France under Napoleon; Germany, twice, under Bismarck and Hitler; Spain under the Spanish Armada; England as the Mistress of the Seas, etc. They've all had their day, never quite making it.

European Scenario

I wanted to start from the Scripture first, to give an overview. I'd like to highlight briefly what most people are not really sensitive to as to what's been going on in Europe over the last three decades. After the Second World War, Europe was in shambles. The leadership in Europe knew they could never allow that to happen again. They felt that for the security of Europe, they would have to unite. Many attempts to do it directly failed. There was too much animosity, too many other problems. But a group of far-sighted visionaries felt that the way you would unite Europe is to unite its economy first, and the way you start that is with a heavy industry. And in 1951, a treaty was signed called the Treaty of Paris. They created a strange entity called the European Coal and Steel Community, a common market in coal and steel. Six nations signed it, but the primary players were

France and Germany. It was a very strange entity; it created a multi-national commission. It turned out to be very successful and became the model of a subsequent treaty. March 25, 1957 (effective January 1, 1958), they signed a treaty in Rome. These same six countries signed a series of treaties collectively called the Treaty of Rome. It created two other entities: The European Atomic Energy Community and the European Economic Community, creating a common effort in atomic energy and also a common effort in developing a customs union and economic interests.

If you study this carefully, and you read the press, in those days they thought this was a fanciful, nonsensical venture that had no chance of success. Well, to make a long story short, of course, it has been quite successful. It has not been quick. It's been ahead of schedule, incidentally, but it has not been quick. On March 19, 1958, a European Parliament was established. That surprises many people. Many people to this day do not realize that there is a parliament of Europe. In 1959, three of the nations combined into what they call the BeNeLux group: Belgium, Luxembourg, and the Netherlands. But in 1967, something interesting happened that most people in this country, including the press, didn't pay attention to. At that time, there were three commissions, three entities in Europe: the Atomic Energy Community, the European Economic Community, and the original Coal and Steel Community, that all had substantial organizations. They merged into one, and in July of 1967 this became what's properly called the European Community. It's interesting to this very day that the press still speaks of the Common Market. That's an out-of-date idiom as of July 1967.

In about 1973, Denmark, Ireland, and the United Kingdom joined; Greece, Spain, and Portugal also joined subsequently, so the original six are joined by six more, making 12. And today we hear a lot about the EC 12. But don't fall into the trap of presuming that when you talk about Europe, you're talking just about the EC 12. The press generally does; even sophisticated financial publications fail to understand what's really going on. There is a group of nations not part of the EC 12. The EC 12 today consists of France, Germany, Italy, and the three BeNeLux countries, Netherlands, Belgium, Luxembourg — that's the original bunch, and Britain, Ireland, Denmark, Greece, Spain, and Portugal. There are a group of nations known as the EFTA (European Free Trade Association) nations: Iceland, Norway, Finland, Sweden, Austria, Switzerland, and Liechtenstein. Six of these seven have announced openly they are joining the EC. So you had the original six, you got another six, and you've got six more joining. I mention that because everybody likes groups of sixes. Don't make too much of that, because there's a few more going to join, too, so the pattern breaks. But the point is Switzerland of the EFTA nations has decided to stay out, but the other six are joining. So the European Community is going to grow substantially. It's a question of legislators and legislative actions and other things.

Now, why am I getting into all of this? Because the European Community, extended, represents an economy and a population base larger than the United

States. The United States has had a policy to encourage this because we had the idea from the way it's been presented that we're creating a democratic, capitalistic, Atlantic trading partner. That's utter nonsense. Europe is socialistic, protectionist, anti-American, pro-Islamic. There are 16 million Muslims in the group. There are more Muslims in Britain than there are Christians. We need to recognize that the style, direction, and policies of the European Community are really quite diverse from what ours would be. It's interesting that we have created not so much a trading partner, but a very powerful competitor.

Now, this is not new news. I can remember in May of 1967, I was in the Ford Motor Company board room, and Sir John Andrews was presenting to the executives assembled the 30-year strategy of the Ford Motor Co., the long-term strategy. Sir John Andrews is about to retire as vice president international, and he had busied himself for 10 years, developing the broad brush corporate strategy for Ford. He felt that the economies of planet Earth would be controlled from Europe in the foreseeable horizon. He proposed that the Ford Motor Co. center its corporate strategies around Europe. Now you have to understand what he was proposing was manifestly illegal. We had about 60,000 employees in Dunton, England, at that time, Ford of Britain; we had about 40,000 employees in Port of Cologne, Germany, and when you opened a plant in Europe, the prime minister would attend. It was a big deal. The other boards were primarily marketing organizations.

What John Andrews was proposing was that

we integrate operations in Europe. Build all the engines in one place, all the transmissions in another. And the only thing that would be unique to each country would be the exterior sheet metal and the marketing organizations. Now that all happens to be illegal, because you don't fool around with transfer prices across sovereign borders. Well, he went through his presentation and I think everybody in the room, certainly the finance staff, a staff representing a 3,000-man organization, all thought John Andrews had gone senile, that this made no sense. "Now that we've heard the presentation, fine; let him retire and let us get back to business."

There were two guys in the room who didn't feel that way. One was Henry Ford II, whose name was on the building, and the other was R.J. Miller III, the president of the company and my boss. Thirty days later, they announced Ford of Europe. There were about 200 attorneys who worked day and night to keep it legal. In the United States, General Motors dominated Ford by about two to one. In Europe, Ford dominated General Motors by two to one, because they also own a lot of other companies in Europe. Many of us don't understand what the word "multi-national" really means. It's not a company that does a lot of export and import, but a company that in many ways actually straddles borders. The largest exporter out of Japan is an organization called IBM. IBM manages the western hemisphere from Tokyo, all but the continental U.S. These are multi-national corporations. Many of them are larger than most governments. If you don't believe that, look at IBM's losses lately.

What I'm trying to paint a picture of here is that the European super-state that's emerging across the Atlantic is not a sudden thing. The smart money has seen it coming. I personally watched it for 30 years, coming like a glacier. Not smoothly; with lots of problems.

It's interesting to watch Germany. For 40 years, everybody worked hard for something they knew would never happen: the unification of Germany. Now that it's happened, everybody's terrified. Of course, western Germany trying to swallow East Germany's costs is a big problem. And they certainly have difficulties. Yet when you start looking at demographics, one of the things that I would encourage is a study of what's called the "heartland concepts." As a Naval Academy graduate, both West Point and Annapolis, I've spent a lot of time on global strategy and geopolitics. One of the things that we get briefed on is global geopolitics. When we were in the Second World War, just to give you an example of what I'm talking about, we were faced with a two-front war. We had Hitler in Europe and we had the Japanese in the Pacific, and we had a problem: We couldn't fight two simultaneously. That's a sure way to lose. We had to pick one and nail it first. The heartland concept demonstrates that if you can control the heartland of Europe, you can control the resources of the planet Earth. If Hitler could have consolidated his gains in Europe, it would have been over. So the number one priority was to neutralize Hitler. We put a token effort in the Pacific until that was done; once Hitler was neutralized, then we shifted our major forces into the

Pacific, all because of the heartland concept. From that background, it fascinated me to watch all of this, because we see Europe moving.

What also has come out of Europe is this whole concept of globalism. The idea is that earth suffers from problems that are global, not regional: over-population, global warming, etc. The big one, of course, is nuclear proliferation.

Globalism

You and I will hear a lot about globalism. We'll hear a lot of rationales, or why this planet needs to be moving towards a global government. We've heard some of them already. Let me tell you the one that I believe will be the forcing function to make it happen. You don't hear much about it. That's nuclear proliferation. You and I have enjoyed nuclear stability for almost five decades because of a doctrine called "Mutually Assured Destruction," based on three pre-suppositions: There are only two players, they're both in balance, and they're both rational. Classic stand-off. It worked. Not very popular in the press, but it did work. Let's look at it today. How many players, how many Third World countries have nuclear capability? The answer is 11. And by the way, how many countries are building inter-continental ballistic missiles today? The answer is 22 — and they're all mad at each other.

The second presupposition, only two players, both in balance. Hardly. There is a race going on. Rafsanjani of Iran has purchased nuclear weapons on the black market. And these are not rumors. I had dinner with a guy who was responsible for checking the bank accounts in Luxembourg and Germany that were used. The first Muslim who can lob a nuclear weapon into Israel will be a hero for eternity in their world. It's a race.

The third presupposition is that they're both rational. You're talking about radical Muslim interests here. How do you have a chicken race with someone who believes he goes to heaven if he loses?

What's the answer? I don't believe we should be stripping down our military, of course. But suppose you went the other way and had a military 10 times the size of our present one. What would you do with it? At whom would you point it? You see, the problem is global supervision.

In Europe, there's been a lot of writing about this over the decades. There is an organization called the Club of Rome, who funded studies, sort of a think-tank, brain-trust-type group. If you'll follow these documents, you'll notice that they all presume that there will be a global government. The real challenge before mankind is how do you get there nonviolently? And the ultimate scenarios fall into three groups. The first class is called the imperialist scenario, or one nation becomes strong enough to impose its will on the rest. Most writers believe that's obsolete in today's technology. So it's a classic historical pattern, but it's not likely for the future. Second class of scenarios, that's the multi-national scenario. That's where all the nations get together and agree. We tried that with the League of Nations, it didn't quite work. The UN has, in general, been that kind of a thing. The U.S. has tried to prop it up through the Persian Gulf maneuvers, etc., and there are many who still believe that maybe the UN will grow into what we're talking about. But there's a third class of scenarios. And that's where a group of nations get together, and they become powerful enough to impose their will on the rest. Well, that group is in a federal union scenario. That's a little more interesting. Because we can think of 13 colonies that started that idea and didn't do too badly for the better part of two centuries. And that's what's happening in Europe. These nations are getting together. France and Germany are pooling their military. Can you believe that? Have they no history books?

There is an agenda that is anticipating a global government. And it may very well be that the real power may be driven by the interests in the U.S. who are agitating in that direction. But despite all of that, I personally plan to stand back and watch very carefully the Europeans. Because as I read the Scripture, Daniel 2 and 7, and as I read Revelation, which ties to that so intimately, I can't help but feel that when the smoke finally clears, the final power group that really calls the shots will be Euro-centered. Not limited to Europe; global, yes. But Euro-centered.

And while this is going on, we see two superpowers on the rise: Europe is emerging as a superstate. Major, major portions of the United States' economic wherewithal is controlled by the European bankers. Many feel that our financial policies will increasingly be dictated by those European bankers. Then, of course, Asia is on the rise. The world is really changing. And you can always win if you know what the rules are. So part of the challenge to you and me as the world changes so dramatically and so quickly is to perceive those changes, to recognize the changes happening, and to understand the basic, broad trends that are impacting us.

But as we do so, we have an advantage over the other analysts. You and I have an advantage in that we have the end written from the beginning in the Bible. This is the time to do your homework and find out what the Bible says about Europe, the city of Babylon, Israel, Jerusalem, the temple and Magog. And in all of this recognize that you and I are plunging into a period of time about which the Bible says a great deal.

Remember that we're not talking about a single issue. Every one of them is climaxing before our very eyes. When I was in the Naval Academy, we learned a proverb, and I think those of you who are sailors have probably heard this: "Red sky at night, sailor's delight. Red sky in the morning, sailor take warning." When I was in the Naval Academy, I knew that was an old proverb, but I had no idea how old. It's in Matthew 16. It was an old proverb that Jesus called upon. He says, "You say this, and you can discern the weather. But you can't discern the signs of the time." He held them accountable to know what times they lived in. You and I can talk about the signs of the times, but I think it's more descriptive to point out that you and I live in the times of the signs. The Old Testament, the New Testament, the entire Bible, details specific things that we are specifically charged to understand when they happen. The rise of a superstate in Europe is but one of them.

6

America at the Crossroads: Freedom or Slavery

Don McAlvany

Revelation 13:16-18 says, "And he caused all, both small and great, rich and poor, free and bond, to receive a mark in their right hand or in their foreheads: And that no man might buy or sell, save he that had the mark, or the name of the beast, or the number of his namc. Hcrc is wisdom. Let him that hath understanding count the number of the beast, for it is the number of a man; and his number is 666."

In all Communist countries, the citizens or slaves must carry identification papers on their person at all times and must be ready to present their papers to Communist authorities at all times — at border checkpoints, at train or bus stations, airport roadblocks, etc. Every citizen fears the ominous words, "Show me your papers." Lacking computerization, it was a way of life.

The Emerging National ID Card

The new national identification card being discussed by the U.S. government will be a computerized card that carries up to 2,000 pages of information on each citizen. The government has proposed three separate ID cards, but all are likely to be ultimately merged into one all-purpose card.

The U.S. Department of Immigration and Naturalization Service has their national card, a single, tamper-resistant INS card for all Americans, including your Social Security number, photo, fingerprints, and barcode to verify employment eligibility. This card will be linked to a nationwide government database and will allegedly solve the problem of illegal aliens getting jobs. It seems a bit fishy to me that they're planning to track 260 million Americans so that they can allegedly watch out for only one million aliens. Mark Rowdenburg, Director of the Electronic Privacy Information Center, said in *USA Today* that it will become a way to monitor people like an eternal passport. This Orwellian nightmare will, like the government's privacy bank cash reporting laws, allow the government to monitor 260 million Americans that are not illegal aliens just as they monitor the cash transactions of 260 million Americans who are not drug dealers.

The second major card is the national health care card. Although it failed in its first try, expect it to be back. One of the major benefits of the socialized medicine program is to get a national ID card in the hand of every American. This high-tech ID card is designed to keep government-accessible records of all aspects of your healthcare, including the details of every doctor visit, every drug store prescription, and every hospital treatment. To make this tracking system work, every one of us must have a number that can be fed into a national computer databank. That's why a National Health Board was necessary: to assign 18-digit identification numbers for each American. The first nine numbers are assumed to be your Social Security number.

When the national health care bill finally passes, you must use the card by law, or not be allowed to receive medical service in America.

The third card comes via the U.S. Postal Service. This general-purpose smart card is most likely to emerge as America's new national ID card, incorporating all the functions of the INS and medical cards, and much more. The postal service was directed by the Department of Defense to develop a people-monitoring electronic card. It recently unveiled a general purpose U.S. services smart card. An individual's card would be automatically connected to the Department of Health and Human Services, the U.S. Treasury, the IRS, the Veteran's Administration, and all other government agencies like the ATF, FBI, CIA, OSHA, FDA, etc. The next link would be to tie it to the banking system and a central databank.

The postal service has acknowledged that it is prepared to put more than 100 million of these cards into citizens' pockets within months of the administration's approval of the program. In other words, they are further along than we thought. This means the project for the computerized control over all Americans is not only on the fast track, it's much further advanced than most people suppose. It's not being done with congressional approval, but rather, through a series of presidential executive orders.

The IRS, not wanting to be left behind, is aggressively pursuing plans for an identity card for taxpayers. There would be one U.S. card for every member of your family. In the not-too-distant future, you are likely to find a harmless-looking smart card in the mail in an official-looking envelope.

Eventually, regardless of what you call it, you won't be able to own property, receive government benefits, get medical attention, or conduct bank or credit card transactions without the card. Executive orders have already been drafted to adopt the cards and force them on the American people with or without congressional approval. (They probably will get congressional approval before it's all over.)

This whole people-control smart card project was birthed by U.S. security agencies who were simply using the Postal Service/INF/health care program as a cover. The Defense Department is already deploying the system at this time, presumably to work out the kinks.

The word tessera as in the tessera smart card has an interesting Latin origin. It means "a piece of mosaic." It is the name given by ancient Roman conquerors to identify chips that they issued to conquered peoples and slaves. It was adopted as the code name for the smart card development project apparently by the defense department. The U.S. card is designed to mediate information about you like a magic key in every government database that contains information about you.

William Murray, an information systems security consultant, said in a *Digital Media* article in May, 1994, entitled, "Ever Feel You're Being Watched? You Will," "There won't be anything you do in business that won't be collected and analyzed by the government. This national information infrastructure is a better surveillance mechanism than Orwell or the government could have ever imagined. This thing is so pervasive in the propensity to connect it, so great that it is unstoppable." Murray continued, "Most of this shift in privacy policy is apparently done by executive order at the initiative of the bureaucracy and without any congressional oversight or concurrence. They are not likely to fail. You know, Orwell said that bureaucrats, simply doing what bureaucrats do, without motive or intent, will use technology to enslave the people." But there is motivation and intent; it is called people-control. It is called the New World Order.

Then there is the MARC card. The MARC card, a prototype to the national ID card, is already being used by the U.S. military. The MARC card, which means Multi-Technology Automated Reader Card is a smart card now being issued by the Department of the Defense to U.S. military personnel. This smart card uses a magnetic stripe, embossed data, printed information, including a digital photograph, and an integrated circuit computer chip. The Department of Defense Information Technology Board initiated the MARC project several years ago to have the ability to instantly track and control all U.S. military personnel worldwide. It is the prototype for the national ID card to be issued to every member of the U.S. civilian population. The MARC card will store all medical information on you and much more.

Included on this so-called MARC card is all your medical information. On each card carrier, in its integrated circuit chip, it will store all personal information, all legal information, all family information, all personal data, all educational background, any police records, your religious background, etc. The DOD considers one of the most important aspects of the MARC system to be its ability to continually track the location of each cardholder worldwide. The carrier cannot get his or her meals at military bases or installations, or buy food or other goods at base exchanges without the card, which also carries all the medical data on the carrier. A person cannot get access to military treatment facilities without the card. It hasn't been issued to everyone yet in the military, but it's making its way to all the bases.

One of the more advanced cards is the laser card. The laser optical memory card produced by Drexler Technology Corporation/Laser Card Systems Corporation is an updatable, credit-card sized, multi-megabyte, data storage card used for storing up to 1,600 pages, 4.1 megabytes of information, on the carrier. It is based on optical recording technology, the process of writing and reading with light. It says on the back that you can actually hold up to 2,000 pages of information on it about you, and of course, you'll never be able to leave home without it. The laser optical memory card is a recordable, security computer readable, data storage card for accumulating and carrying up to 2,000 pages of information. A single card holds three megabytes of text and software, over four megabytes of digitized graphics, voice, and image. And, of course, when you go around and you hand it to somebody at a checkpoint or whatever, they simply put it in the machine, and all this information about you comes rolling out. Isn't that going to be fun?

The card has ample memory to store personal identification numbers, PINs, digital photos, signatures, voice prints, fingerprints, hand geometry, and virtually all personal biographic data on the card holder. It can store text, graphics, voice pictures, software, virtually any form of information that can be digitized.

Drexler, AT&T, and a host of other high-tech research development and production companies are working closely with DOD and other departments of the U.S. government to develop cards like the MARC card and the emerging new national ID smart card. Drexler says in its literature that it can produce up to 40 million laser cards per year and the postal service says that it can distribute up to 100 million such cards in a matter of just a few months.

Is the national ID smart card the first step to an implanted biochip? The new government ID cards are a devious new means of further consolidating and computerizing all available information on each of us into a new, electronically digitized, centralized government database that will ultimately lead to a complete loss of privacy, enslavement, and control. To make this enslaving system work, each of us must have a unique ID number that can be fed into various local, national, and international computer databanks. That is why the National Health Board would be necessary to enforce, in their words, "unique identification numbers for all consumers." This is already being done in Canada.

The national identity card, whether it takes the form of a national health card, electronic benefits card, or whatever, will become so necessary in order to comply with various government regulations that we will be forced to carry it with us at all times. But that leads to obvious problems: What if we lose it? What if someone steals it? Would we be able to function without it? Probably not. The New World Order government has a solution. You see, there is a new, more advanced and sophisticated system of identification that cannot be lost or stolen. It will eventually make the ID card obsolete. It is a syringe-implantable ID transponder biochip that goes into your body. The tiny microchip, only the size of a grain of rice, is simply injected under the skin of your right hand. These tiny transponders are presently being injected into pets, cattle, sheep, goats, and other livestock by veterinarians and ranchers all across

America as a means of computerized identification and location of a lost or stolen animal.

The newest of these tiny transponders are now being reduced to about one-sixth the size of a grain of rice, or about the size of a splinter. You can very easily inject it under the skin of your pet animal or under your own skin. Several years ago the DOD began to experiment with tiny, microchip implants in GI's fillings in lieu of dog tags. These relatively simple biochip radio receiver implants are battery-free, passive devices that will have everyone's unalterable, international, 18-digit ID number electronically encoded into them. Once they have been injected under our skin, we will have been electronically branded for life. Liken it to a modern electronic technological tattoo, if you will; without accepting it, no one will be permitted to buy or sell anything anywhere in the coming cashless, global economy.

This technology seems to already be tested and will be applied and implemented over the next 5 or 10 years. Some people would argue sooner, and the program could be accelerated if necessary — like in a national emergency.

In the coming New World Order system of socialist-type control, there will be no jobs, no food, no homes, no cars, no health care, no welfare or food stamps, no retirement benefits, no bank accounts or money without this high-tech electronic ID mark in your body. You will not be able to function in any respect whatsoever without the world government ID debit chip implant. Nor will you have any individual privacy. It will have been eliminated.

The transponder ID-debit chips will not only replace cash, checks, and credit cards; they will supplant all existing forms of identification. The implants will become our passports, drivers' licenses, credit cards, ATM cards, health care cards, Social Security cards, etc. In other words, they will become our universal ID and ATM debit chips, all in one. One world, one biochip. AT&T presently advertises its new contactless electronic card as "One world, one card." Isn't that nice?

With the new chip implant you simply pass your right hand over a radio frequency scanner and you will be identified instantly and processed automatically wherever you are. The radio wave will pass through the skin of your hand, activate your ID transponder, and transmit your unique ID number back outside the skin to the scanner. This entire process will take less than two seconds. Computers in the new, digitized, fiber-optical information superhighway infrastructure will do the rest. I'm sure you've been reading about the information superhighway and saying, "Boy, isn't this a wonderful, wonderful thing." Yes, and it's talked about in the Book of Revelation.

Tim Willard, executive officer of the World Future Society, a Washington, DC-based New Age organization that claims 27,000 members globally, including *Future Shock* author Alvin Toffler, was quoted in 1989 as saying, "The technology behind such a biochip implant is fairly simple, fairly uncomplicated, and with a little refinement, could be used in a variety of human applications. Conceivably, a number could be assigned at birth and follow that person throughout life. Most likely, it would be implanted on the back of the right hand or left hand so that it could be easy to scan in stores. Then you could simply scan your hand to automatically debit your bank account." Willard added, "The biochip implant could also be used as a universal type of identification card that would replace all credit cards, passports, and that sort of thing. It could also become our medical card, ID chip, it could even replace house and car keys some day." It would be very convenient.

Martin Anderson, a senior fellow at the Hoover Research Institute at Stanford University in Palo Alto, California, and a former high-ranking official in the Reagan administration, said in an April 7, 1993, article in the San Jose *Mercury,* "Unless this move to force a national identity card on Americans is stopped quickly, we may live to see the end of all privacy in the United States. All of us will be tagged like so many fish." In another article by Anderson, October 4, 1993, in the *Washington Times,* he said this about the ID biochip implant in our bodies: "There is an identification system made by Hughes Aircraft Company that, unlike your national identity card, you cannot lose. It's the syringe-implantable transponder." He goes on, "According to promotional literature, this is an ingenious, safe, inexpensive, fool-proof, and permanent method of identification using radio waves. A tiny microchip the size of a grain of rice is simply placed under the skin. It is so designed as to be injected simultaneously or with a vaccination or alone."

Wouldn't it be something — as they force

vaccinations on all children in America starting with the passage of the U.N. Convention on the Rights of the Child and other legislation now floating around in Washington — while giving your children a shot, decided to slip in a little splinter. You'd never know; won't bother them. Won't hurt them. It'll just be there for future use.

Anderson goes on, "This tiny microchip transponder is like a technological tattoo, and far more effective than the numbers the Nazis marked indelibly on the arms of the concentration camp victims. There is no difference in principle between being forced to carry a microchip and a plastic ID card in your wallet or in a little transponder pellet injected in your arm. The principle that Big Brother has the right to track you is inherent in both; the only thing that differentiates the two techniques is a layer of your skin."

Currently, farmers, pet owners, and manufacturers are using radio frequency biochips or transponders to track and control their animals and equipment. But one day soon, every human being on earth may also be tracked and controlled in a like manner using this technology. In the coming New World Order's global government, we will all have become assets of the establishment.

Conclusion: The national ID card is almost a reality and could be implemented within 6 to 12 months, by executive orders from our President, making a total end-run around the U.S. Congress. Technology has now perfected the physical capacity to produce hundreds of millions of these cards and link them to presently existing government databases. With the significant year 2000 only a few years away, the establishment is moving toward the national ID people-control system at Mach 10 speed.

Could the national ID card be a steppingstone to a computerized biochip transponder? The technology for this now exists and the people-controlled motives of our leaders seem, at least to me, to be very clear. The whole concept of a national ID smart card and implantable biochip seem far-out, bizarre, implausible, and like something out of science fiction. Except for one thing: Our government is working feverishly to develop such people-control systems right now.

Loss of Privacy

Let's look at the American people under surveillance.

America today is becoming rapidly a total surveillance society and privacy as we have known it, since the founding fathers, is now being abolished. Our government has been pushing hard for a number of people-controlling, people-monitoring, high-tech systems, including the national ID card, the national information superhighway, installation of a federal clipper chip in our telephones, computers, fax machines, and other electronic machines to allow government tapping and monitoring of all communications through those devices.

Attorney General Janet Reno has argued that to stop terrorism and organized crime, the American people must give up some of their personal freedom and privacy. Really? Isn't that interesting. Phone, cable, and computer network companies will have to modify their switches and computers to ensure that surveillance can be conducted concurrently from a remote government facility. All transactions and phone calls in and out will be monitored and recorded. The Electronic Frontier Foundation has warned, "The FBI scheme would turn the data superhighway into a national surveillance network of staggering proportions."

The clipper chip surveillance will enable Big Brother bureaucracy to monitor every phone call, every credit card purchase, every bank transaction, and every telecommunication of every private citizen in America. The *Wall Street Journal* in July 1994 wrote the following: "The potential for government manipulation and intimidation of the citizenry is enormous."

One of the essential elements of the New World Order is the need for a cashless society. All transactions would be handled through a computerized banking and credit card system and, eventually, through an all-purpose national ID smart card. One-hundred percent monitoring and control of all personal activity is the goal and could become a reality over the next five to 10 years. If you are determined to be politically incorrect, Big Brother can withhold or tie-up transactions until you conform.

The backers of the New World Order know they can't get all of this approved through Congress. Instead, most of the work is approved executive orders. This avoids alarming the public when developing people-control elements. They simply write an executive order and use these highly unconstitutional dictatorial-type powers to accomplish their end.

Executive orders dating back to Franklin Delano Roosevelt give the president the ability to declare a state of emergency, martial law, suspension of all constitutional rights, and establish a total dictatorship with the stroke of a pen. Executive orders are recorded in the Federal Register and therefore accepted by Congress as the law of the land which can be implemented at the whim of the president in an emergency, which he can declare.

Some examples of executive orders already on the books:

#10995, All communications media can be seized by the federal government.

#10997, The government can seize all electrical power and fuels, including gasoline and minerals.

#10998, Seizure of all food resources, farms, and farm equipment.

#10999, Seizure of all types of transportation (including your personal car), control of highways and seaports.

#11000, Seizure of all civilians for work under federal supervision.

#11001, Federal takeover of all health, education and welfare.

#11002, The postmaster general is empowered to register every man, woman, and child in the USA.

#11003, Seizure of all aircraft and airports.

#11004, Housing and finance authority may shift population from one locality to another.

#11005, Seizure of railroads, inland waterways, and storage facilities.

#11051, The director of the Office of Emergency Planning is authorized to put executive orders into effect in times of increased international tension or financial crisis.

Congress has granted all these powers, without checks and balances, to the president of the United States. In short, if there should be a nationwide riot, or a national financial crisis, massive social upheaval, a quantum increase in crime, major resistance to national gun confiscation or to the installation of the New World Order or other socialist police state measures, the president has the power, and machinery, to instantly suspend the Constitution and declare a total dictatorship. The president determines if these emergency powers are needed. Would he do such a thing? You tell me. America needs to understand the importance of who they are electing as president.

Is there a concerted effort to attack Christians and traditionalists? Joseph Stalin said, "America is like a healthy body and its resistance is threefold: its patriotism, its morality and its spiritual life. If we can undermine these three areas, America will collapse from within."

Samuel Adams said, "While the people are virtuous they cannot be subdued; but when they once lose their virtue, they will be ready to surrender their liberties to the first external or internal invader." Have we, as a country, lost our virtue? Look around.

Don't Like Christians

Evangelical Christians and people espousing traditional values have never been popular among the political left, those most committed to bring the world together under a one world government. The liberals in the government, the judiciary, the media, the educational system, the arts, the entertainment industry, all have been unchecked in their ability to draw up a New World Order transition. Since 1960 they've taken prayer and any mention of God out of the public schools and out of public life. They have totally denigrated Christians and traditionalists on television, in movies, in books, and in the print media, which is now beginning to portray Christians and traditionalists as a dangerous threat to the nation.

They have filled the media with quotes like, "Waco should be a warning to dangerous religious cults that the same thing can happen to them." No one gave the government the right to come in and gas and burn those people just because their beliefs were different, even if they were suspected of crimes. There is due process.

The establishment press began to describe how you could recognize a dangerous religious cult or cultist by portraying fundamental Christians as radical types who are hung up on Bible prophecy, preoccupied with the imminent second coming of Jesus Christ. They view world events in relation to the Armageddon scenario. Many of them are home schoolers who believe in the right to gun ownership. Most are child abusers because they spank their children. Their dangerous beliefs in the past have contributed to the Cold War, the arms race and at present are contributing to poverty, crime, gang warfare, divisiveness, homophobia, overpopulation of the planet, and pollution of Mother Earth. Basically the media is defining Christian fundamentalists as those who are destroying the nation and something has to be done about it.

The liberals have recently launched an attack against Christian conservatives via an effort to outlaw the mention of God in the workplace on penalty of fines, business closures, or jail.

While most Americans are slapping high fives over electing a Republican majority in Congress, take a look at the new regulations they are trying to push through the Equal Employment Opportunity Commission. Items and actions to be banned at the workplace: wearing a cross around the neck, wrist, or any openly visible part of the body, wearing a yamaka, displaying a picture of Christ on an office wall or desk, wearing a t-shirt, hat, or other clothing that has any religious emblem on it, displaying a Bible or other religious books on a desk or otherwise making the same openly visible in a work or lounge area. Also targeted are the hosting of Christmas, Hanukkah, Thanksgiving, or Easter celebrations, parties, or events in any form that have any focus on Christ, God, or other religious connotations; celebrations or parties in any form which have any religious focus or reference; opening or closing prayer or invocation at a company program, banquet, celebration, or event; witnessing the gospel, sharing your faith, and generally speaking to other employees about religion; Nativity scenes or displays; inviting a fellow employee to a synagogue, church, temple, or other place of worship. Also, conversations about religion or religious groups; functions, and events; prayer breakfasts; singing or humming a religious song while at a copy machine; serving only pork or beef at a company Fourth of July picnic; having a local church choir or school choir come in for a Christmas celebration and sing any songs which make reference to Christ, God, or any religion or religious principle; Christmas carols; telling any joke, regardless of the innocence or intent of the matter, that refers to any religion or religious group whatsoever; giving a fellow employee a holiday card, birthday card, get well, greeting card, or plaque which includes any religious reference; making reference to Christ, God, or any religious figure or subject matter in a company mission, plan, or goal statement; praying while in the workplace; the display of calendars with thoughts of the day, books which make reference to Scripture or religious sayings; displaying any religious artwork, devotional figure, symbol, or trinket in an openly visible area; hosting a Bible study or other religious gathering; almost any form of religious expression in the workplace.

In the 1960s, school prayer was eliminated. Since then, invocations at a graduation have been banned. Christmas decorations and caroling are out. And even voluntary student-initiated activities, like Bible study groups, take a court order.

U.N. Convention on the Rights of the Child

This dangerous United Nations treaty, already ratified and therefore the law of the land in 150 countries, will allow the government, or the world government, under the United Nations New World Order, to dictate how you raise your children, what you can and cannot do and the role that the state will have in raising your children. If ratified, the U.N. Convention on the Rights of the Child will be implemented in the United States and virtually destroy the parental rights we presently enjoy. This treaty will give all children the right to freedom of association, freedom of expression, freedom of religion, the right to privacy (which includes the right to abortion), the right to choose public schools, the right to access the media (including TV), basically they choose what's good for them, not their parents.

Any parent who infringed on his or her children's rights in these areas can be prosecuted with penalties of jail or having their children removed from the home. This treaty virtually prohibits corporal punishment of children. Spanking of children will be in the same category as criminal child abuse. Such child abusers may be jailed and have their children taken from them. In France, in the first few days following the ratification of the treaty, seven families had their children taken from them and the parents were jailed for the new international crime of child abuse, that is, spanking their children.

Many millions of Christians and Jews worldwide follow biblical teachings on child discipline. It couldn't be worded more clearly in the Bible:

> He who spares his rod hates his son, But he who loves him disciplines him diligently (Prov. 13:24).

> Foolishness is bound up in the heart of a child; The rod of discipline will remove it far from him (Prov. 22:15).

> Do not hold back discipline from the child, Although you beat him with the rod, he will not die (Prov. 23:13).

> The rod and reproof give wisdom, But a child who gets his own way brings shame to his mother (Prov. 29:15).

The impact of the convention is particularly ominous in light of the fact that the United States Constitution declares treaties to be the law of the land. Thus, the U.S. Convention would constitute legally binding laws in all 50 states. Otherwise valid state laws pertaining to education, the family, etc., which conflict with the provisions of the treaty, will be subject to invalidation.

Senate Resolution 70 has been circulated since mid-1983. Presently around 50 senators are on record as co-sponsors calling for President Clinton to send the U.N. Convention on the Rights of the Child to the Senate for ratification. It only takes 16 more. Over 150 groups have indicated their support for the U.N. Convention on the Rights of the Child, including the National Education Association, the National Council for Social Services, the National Committee for the Rights of the Child, Planned Parenthood of New York, International School Boards Association, American Bar Association, International Council on Social Welfare, and the Girl Scouts of America.

• Summary of the Articles of Convention:

Article 3 — In all actions concerning children, the courts, social service workers, and bureaucrats are empowered to regulate families based on their subjective determination of "the best interest of the child." This shifts the responsibility of parental judgment or decision-making from the family to the state and ultimately to the United Nations.

Article 4 — Nations are required to undertake all appropriate legislative, administrative and other measures for the implementation of the rights of the Convention. In fact, the U.S. would be required to undertake measures to the maximum extent of available resources within a framework of international cooperation in order to restructure society. This is not just about children; it's about restructuring our whole country under U.N. law.

Article 7 — All children will be immediately registered to ensure state and U.N. control over their development. In case you didn't realize it, when you have a baby today, before it leaves, it is being registered for a social security number at the hospital. But now they're going to be registered internationally under this treaty.

Article 13 — Parents will be subject to prosecution for any attempt to prevent their children from interaction with pornography, rock music, or television. Little children are vested with the freedom of expression. It is virtually absolute with no allowance made for parental guidance. Article 14 — Children are guaranteed freedom of thought, conscience, and religion. They can object to all religious training. They can assert their right to participate in a cult or contrary services.

Article 15 — The right of the child to freedom of association. If taken seriously, parents would be prevented from forbidding their child to associate with people deemed to be objectionable companions. Children could claim this right and join gangs, cults, racist organizations, and associate with drug addicts over parental objections. Parental rights and responsibilities are not mentioned.

Article 16 — Mandates the creation of an intensive bureaucracy with the purpose of identification reporting for full investigation, treatment, and follow-up of parents, who in the violation of children's rights, treat their children negligently.

Article 24 — The governments of each signatory nation are required to provide the highest standard of health care facilities, including family planning and education services.

Article 26 — Parties must recognize the right of every child to benefit from Social Security and social insurance so every child from birth must have a Social Security number and be computerized.

Article 27 — Parents are required to implement conditions of living necessary for the child's development. These conditions of living are to be derived from state-determined standards for his or her physical, mental, spiritual, moral, and social development. (Apparently, this gives them the right to come and inspect your home.)

Article 28 — Compulsory education. All nations are challenged to unite in the creation of an internationalist approach to education. All school-age Americans would be encouraged to be part of the school system, the content of what is to be taught to all children is prescribed. These include anti-Americanism, one-worldism, anti-family and anti-traditional values, multiculturalism, environmentalism, including earth worship. The home school movement is dramatically endangered by this convention. It can be attacked or terminated by this article.

Article 29 — It is the goal of the state to direct the education of the people it governs toward the philosophy of the New World Order as enshrined in the charter of the United Nations. This philosophy includes a cultic, anti-Judeo Christian values, authoritarianism and intolerance.

Article 37 — Every child deprived of his or her liberty shall have access to free, legal counsel and access to the courts to make such a challenge. Parents will have to pay new taxes to support the legal process against themselves. Can't you just see the ACLU lawyers standing in line? Article 43 — An international committee of 10 experts is to be established to oversee the progress and implementation of the treaty. These experts will be chosen by secret ballot by all signatory nations. There is no assurance that any American will even be on the committee.

In summary, the Convention would give children the right to disregard parental authority. The state will determine the child's best interests. Provisions of the treaty must be enforced. All children must be registered. Severe limitations are placed on the parents' right to direct and train their children. The Convention would further entrench the rights of teen-agers to have sexual relations and then abort their babies. Parents who don't comply may be prosecuted. It's happening in some of the 150 countries where the treaty has passed. Prohibition of corporal punishment is a key part of it. Our children will be educated for the New World Order world government. International experts will parent our children.

I ask you, should we be waiting for the Rapture to rescue us or should we be motivated to do something? Many other countries have lost their freedoms because they said it could never happen here.

Isaiah 5:20 says, "Woe to those who call evil good and good, evil, who put darkness for light and light for darkness, who put bitter for sweet and sweet for bitter. Woe to those who have put the guilty for a bribe but deny justice to the innocent." Does that not describe America of our day?

Pat Buchanan has said, "What's the Christian-bashing all about? They simply want America to again become the good country that she once was. They want the popular culture to reflect the values that patriotism, loyalty, bravery, and decency used to reflect. They want magazines, movies, and TV shows de-polluted of raw sex, violence, and filthy language. They want the schools for which they pay taxes to believe in the values which they believe. They want their kids to have the same right to pray that they had. And yes, they do want chastity taught as a moral norm and traditional marriage taught as God-ordained, natural, and normal. Is that so wicked and sinister an agenda?"

A struggle for the soul of America is underway, a struggle to determine whose views, values, and standards will serve as the basis of law, who will determine what is right and wrong in America. And that intensifying assault on the Christian right should be taken as a sign that these folks are very serious. Expect the attacks against the Christian traditionalists to accelerate. We know who we believe in and he told us who we are really against. In the inaugural words of Bill Clinton, they are trying to "force the spring on America," a term from wiccan witchcraft. As Ephesians 6:12 says, "For our struggle is not against flesh and blood, but against the rulers, against the authorities, against the powers of this dark world and against the spiritual forces of evil in the heavenly realm."

"This is what the Lord says: 'Stand at the crossroads and look; ask for the ancient paths, ask where the good way is, and walk in it, and you will find rest for your souls. But you said, "We will not walk in it" ' " (Jer. 6:16).

Pray for wisdom and guidance. Proverbs 27:12 says, "The prudent see danger and take refuge but the simple keep going and suffer for it."

I think we need to get angry. We have let evil people come in. They are intent on destroying our traditional values, our Constitution, and our way of life. I encourage you to get involved.

7

Russia Invades Israel: The Explosion Is Near

Chuck Missler

Having been in the class of '56 in the Naval Academy, and having served as chief executive officer of four different defense contractors, I have been provided a background from which I try to maintain our intelligence network that leaks through the newsletter. Hopefully, this background will also provide some complexion to the material that we're going to cover in this chapter.

In the past, I had the privilege of serving on a board with Bill Simon, the former secretary of the treasury; Dr. Edward Teller, who in those days was the principal scientific advisor to President Reagan; and General David C. Jones, who was chairman of the Joint Chiefs of Staff, former general of the air force; and Admiral Tom Hayward, chief of the naval operations who has just retired. All in all, these were probably the best-informed Americans I have had the privilege of communing with.

As an additional side note, I served as chairman of a small, high-technology company which succeeded in signing an $8 billion joint venture with the Soviet Union, a move which gave us KGB sponsorship in and out of the Soviet Union. I mention this because we've had some direct commerce with the old Soviet Union.

It's with this background that I'd like to discuss the Middle East. But first, I prefer to give a secular update from the intelligence community after having some perspective from the Bible. Because for me, the things that are interesting are interesting to the extent that they illuminate the Scripture (or I should be more precise, that the Scripture illuminates for us).

Again, to make clear the peculiar view that I have, is that I see the 66 books of the Bible, written by 40 authors over thousands of years, as an integrated message system. One of the great discoveries is that every number, every place name, every detail is there by design.

I was interested to discover that in Israel, the rabbis have an interesting view of the Torah. They say that we really won't understand the Scriptures until the Messiah comes. But when the Messiah comes, He will not only interpret the passages, He will interpret the very words, He'll even interpret the very letters. In fact, He'll even interpret the spaces between the letters. When I first heard that, I regarded it as sort of a colorful exaggeration until I re-read Matthew 5:17 and 18 where Jesus says, "Think not that I am come to destroy the law, or the prophets: I am not come to destroy, but to fulfill. For verily, I say unto you . . . one jot or one tittle shall in no wise pass from the law, till all be fulfilled." Now, a jot or a tittle are parts of a letter, equivalent in our culture to the crossing of the "t" or the dotting of an "i". And I suddenly realized that these rabbis may be closer to truth than I had realized. Every mistake I've made — and there have been many in the 40 years I've studied the Bible and 20 years I've been teaching it — has been when I didn't take it literally enough.

And so it's at that point of view that I would like to share a little about the most famous passage in the Bible from a prophetic point of view. People who know nothing about Bible prophecy have all heard about Ezekiel 38 and 39, and what I'd like to do is take a quick look at this famous passage.

Who Is Magog?

The word of the Lord came unto me, saying, Son of man, set thy face against Gog, the land of Magog, the chief prince of Meshech and Tubal, and prophesy against him, And say, Thus saith the Lord God; Behold, I am against thee, O Gog, the chief prince of Meshech and Tubal: And I will turn thee back, and put hooks into thy jaws, and I will bring thee forth, and all thine army, horses and horsemen, all of them clothed with all sorts of armour, even a great company with bucklers and shields, and all of them handling swords. Persia, Ethiopia, and Libya with them; all of them with shield and helmet: Gomer, and all his bands; the house of Togarmah of the north quarters, and all its bands; and many people with thee. Be thou prepared, and prepare for thyself, thou, and all thy company that are assembled unto thee, and be thou a guard unto them (Ezek. 38:1-6).

We have here the opening of the chapter that describes an invasion of Israel. And this invasion is led by some people called Magog. Gog is the leader of a group called Magog, and Magog has some allies who are listed. They're going to invade Israel, and this battle is famous for at least two reasons. The first reason it's so well-known among Bible scholars is that it is the occasion God uses to openly intervene in human history. It's famous for another reason because of the apparently explicit description of nuclear weapons, which we'll discuss later.

Have you ever noticed that the Bible always uses strange names? We've got Magog, Gomer, Togarmah, and so forth. Do you know why the Bible always uses these strange names? It's our fault. We keep changing the names of things.

There was a city called Petragrad. Then for many, many years, it was called St. Petersburg. Then for many years, it was called Leningrad. Today, it's called St. Petersburg again. What's it going to be called next year? Nobody knows. My Russian friends tell me that in Russia, even the past is uncertain. There was a city called Byzantium, then it was called Constantinople, and now it's called Istanbul. There was a space center called Cape Kennedy. It's now called Cape Canaverel. We keep changing the names of things.

Well, suppose you were Isaiah, and God told you to talk about the Persian Empire 100 years before it emerges in history. How do you talk about it? Well, you speak about it from the point of view of its ancestors. You simply refer to the ancestors of the Persians. You see, we change the names of cities and nations and things — we generally don't change the name of our ancestors.

All of us are related. And not to Adam alone, but we're all sons of Noah. Noah had three sons, Ham, Shem, and Japheth, and they repopulated the planet Earth. We're all relatives and we're all from Turkey. We're all descendants of Ham, Shem, and Japheth. Their descendants are listed in Genesis 10. Seventy nations are listed there by their tribal names, or the names of the ancestors that derived from the three sons of Noah. This chapter is so foundational to a serious Bible student that it's referred to as the "Table of Nations."

One of the sons of Noah was Japheth, and one of his sons was a guy by the name of Magog. And because of this passage in Ezekiel, Hal Lindsey and I undertook a research project to really nail to the wall the identity of Magog. As we got into this, it became very clear that we had a straw man to knock down because the documentation of who Magog was happens to be very thorough, very complete, and unequivocal. There was a Greek didactic poet in the seventh century, approximately the same time Ezekiel wrote, who identifies Magog as the ancestor of the Scythians. A great deal of the information about the descendants comes from this Greek historian. In fact, he's called "the Father of all History." Herodotus, who wrote about the fifth century, also gives us a great deal of detail about the Scythians, which is the Greek name for the descendants of Magog.

Many have heard of the Great Wall of China. It was described by the ancient Muslim writers and called the "Ramparts of Magog." It was designed to keep the Scythians out. And, obviously, what I'm getting to is that the Scythians are the ancestors to what you would call today the true Russia.

Other Allies

One of the events that all of us obviously have taken note of is the break-up of the Soviet Union. And many of us probably haven't had an opportunity to really explore what that means biblically. It turns out that that break-up sets the stage for Ezekiel 38 in some surprising ways.

The Soviet Union embraced 15 republics that contained 110 ethnic minorities, and they really hated each other. So you begin to sense that constraint has been removed for a while. In the United States, we span four time zones. The Russian Republic alone spans 11. That's just to give a rough feeling of size. Russia is obviously very substantial.

Now what Ezekiel 38 talks about is an invasion by the descendants of Magog (i.e., today we would call them the Russians). The first thing we'll see is that their allies are listed in verse 5. The lead ally, the dominant ally, is somebody called Persia. Who is that today? In 1932 Persia changed it's name to Iran. Cush and Put are the Hebrew terms. Cush settled south of the second cataract of the Nile, and that is one reason why it's typically translated as Ethiopia in the English Bible. That's typically the Roman province of Ethiopia, not the Ethiopia of today, but for practical purposes, connotatively, black Africa. Put settled west of Egypt, and is connotatively used in North Africa.

Gomer, the ancestor of the Samarians and others, settled on the Rhine and Danube valleys. There is also Togarmah. If you know any Armenians today, you know that they, to this day, refer to themselves as the "House of Togarmah." But actually, the descendants of Togarmah also included the Turks. So, we have the complete list of allies.

One of the things that is disturbing about reading biblical commentaries on this passage is that they keep calling these people the Arabs. There's not an Arab among them. That's one of the things I'd like to sensitize you to is that we can talk about Iran, Iraq, Syria, Egypt, Libya, Turkey, and we have not mentioned an Arab yet. In fact, they hate the Arabs, in effect. Now what do we mean by an Arab? If we mean someone genealogically as the son of Ishmael, one of the two sons of Abraham, we've got a problem, because first of all, none of these are sons of Ishmael, but secondly, we exclude the Bedouins. So are we saying a Bedouin is not an Arab? A Bedouin is the son of Keturah, the third wife of Abraham, so it gets complicated. Maybe, then, an Arab is an inhabitant of Ur, of the Arabian peninsula. Possibly, and we'll deal with that a little later.

The point is that these people who are aligned with Magog are not Arabs; in fact, some are sons of Japheth, some Ham, some Shem. They're very diverse ethnologically. What do they have in common? They're all Muslims. They have Islam in common.

Now this allows a short parenthetical update. Let me say that you need to do your homework on Islam. Islam is going to be, I believe, the greatest challenge to Christianity in the nineties. And most people haven't the foggiest notion of what Islam is really all about.

First of all, Islam did not begin with Mohammed. The chief pagan deity in Abraham's day was the moon god. The symbol was the crescent moon. This moon god gets worshipped by many different names throughout history. The Assyrians called him Sin (a strange pun). They called it Sin for King Sinecharid. Sinecharid means "sin multiplies its brothers." The name Sin was an allusion to the moon god. And it's symbol, of course, was the crescent moon. He was, in Abraham's day, the dominant deity among the 360 idols they worshipped then.

When Mohammed comes along, sixth century A.D., and develops his religion, he adopts this pagan god and calls him Allah. It is an Arabic word for god, but it's a very specific god and it's not the God of the Old Testament, like many people presume. And, in fact, the crescent moon that symbolizes the worship of Allah now adorns every mosque around the world.

One to Watch

Most of us have been watching Saddam Hussein in Iraq because of obvious recent history. They founded the Shi-ite sect, the fundamentalist sect of Islam. Saddam Hussein is Sunni, not Shiat. A small percentage of Iraq is Shiat and they happen to be in control, but they're on a slippery rock.

Islam divides the world into two parts. Dar-al Islam, that is, the domain of the faithful, and Dar-al-arb, the domain of those with whom we are at war until judgment day. The goal of Islam is the subjugation of the planet Earth, by the sword if necessary. And it's unfortunate that so many moderates in Islam are destined to be abused by the fact that the extremists are going to work hard to fulfill that goal.

The person to watch in the Middle East, very carefully, is Rafsanjani, the president of Iran. Rafsanjani has announced quite vocally that he believes Islam has replaced Marxism as the ideology of the future. He also has announced that he now has the resources in terms of the oil revenues and the nuclear weapons to disconnect the Middle East from the Judeo-Christian world order. Rafsanjani has succeeded in purchasing nuclear weapons. If Islam has the oil revenues and the nuclear weapons, we cannot any longer ignore their agenda.

Rafsanjani has also announced his grand design, and that's to unite the Islamic world into what he calls an Islamic crescent from the 200 million Muslims in Indonesia all the way to Muratania. Estimates from 1.2 to almost 2 billion Muslims are involved, depending on how you count. We're talking about a formidable force that is growing faster than any other religion on earth.

It's fascinating to see the very line-up that is listed in Ezekiel. In verse 8 we see that there's going to be an invasion. Magog is getting sucked into this invasion. In verse 7, which says, "be thou a guard unto them," the word in the Hebrew implies a provider of weapons, not just a leader. It's interesting that these nations mentioned are armed by whom? Russia — a Third World economy but a first-rate military. They will attack Israel at a time after Israel has been regained from all the nations. If you continue reading from verse 8, looking at verse 12 as an example, they come "to take a spoil, to take a prey, turn thine hand upon the desolate places that are now inhabited upon the people that are gathered out of the nations." Note that the tense is plural; that means it's after the Babylonian captivity. They were regathered twice. First, from Babylon, the second time from the world at large. And we've seen that happen since May 14, 1948. So this invasion occurs after Israel has been regathered in the land.

Ezekiel is an interesting prophet. Here he's describing that after they've been regathered in the land, they're going to be invaded by a group of nations armed and led by Magog, Russia, and you've got Muslim nations involved. It's interesting to notice the nations that are not mentioned. Egypt is not mentioned, conspicuous by its absence, and some others. But we do find the Arabs mentioned. They're not mentioned, like many people think, in Ezekiel 38:5. They're mentioned instead in verse 13. It says, "Sheba, and Dedan, and the merchants of Tarshish, with all the young lions thereof, shall say unto thee, Art thou come to take a spoil? hast thou gathered thy company to take a prey? to carry away silver and gold, to take away cattle and goods, to take a great spoil?" Interesting situation. The Arabs are not invading nor defending. That's a little strange.

Let me insert a little bit of background on Iran. Iran has spent an average of $5 billion a year in the last three years building up its air force. Do you remember those 115 aircraft that flew from Iraq to Iran during the Persian Gulf War? Where are they today? In Iran. Rafsanjani has bought the spares to maintain those aircraft, plus another 110 aircraft. Price tag? $2.2 billion. All made possible because of their oil revenues.

But he's doing something else. He's put his operating forces on maneuvers. They are training, practicing. And as you can imagine, every reconnaissance satellite we've got is watching that closely.

As they practice, we notice something interesting. We notice that they're practicing amphibious operations under conditions of contamination. Iran does not have to have amphibious operations to invade Israel. But it tips us off as to what part of Rafsanjani's strategy includes: invading Saudi Arabia. Why would they do that? They're Muslim too, right? Not quite. They're Sunis.

Actually, Saudi Arabia has done several things that would alienate it from the rest of the so-called Muslim world. First of all, they let us use their real estate during the Persian Gulf War. That's a no-no in Islam. But the real reason is because, in order to accomplish Rafsanjani's goal of the grand design to unite the Islamic world, he has to control Mecca and Medina in their world. No wonder the House of Saud is watching nervously on the sidelines, not invading but not defending. We've spent the last 10 years secretly arming Saudi Arabia for just such a contingency.

I might call your attention to a technicality in verse 16. In that verse, God says, "And thou shalt come up against my people of Israel, as a cloud to cover the land; it shall be in the latter days, and I will bring thee against my land, that the heathen may know me, when I shall be sanctified in thee, O Gog, before their eyes." Interesting; He says, "my land." Whose land is the land of Israel? The God of the universe. Yet it's strange that the God of the universe would single out a piece of real estate and call it His. The earth is the Lord's and the fullness thereof. Indeed. But from Genesis on, He singles out that land as His. His relationship to Abraham, His relationship to the country, Israel, is all tied up in the land. It doesn't belong to the Palestinians, it belongs to the God of the universe.

Also in verse 16, He says something else. "Thou shalt come up against my people of Israel." The naive Bible reader would say, "Well, God always speaks of Israel as 'My people.' " Not true. Study the Book of Hosea. God specifically expresses that there's a period of time when they will be set aside, but not for good. There will be a time when He takes them up again. This phrase is one of the reasons serious Bible scholars would believe that this event occurs after the Church is complete and gone, when God is once again dealing with the earth through the nation of Israel.

What follows in the passage is of course that this invasion by Magog and its allies is going to be intervened in by the Lord himself. He's going to bring an earthquake, and hailstones of fire will fall upon the invading forces.

As a guy who's been in the professional defense establishment for many years (naval academy and air force), I obviously have an interest in battles, and obviously I've been interested in biblical battles. I've made what I think is an interesting observation. There are lots of battles in the Bible, some historical, some prophetic. But in every case that I can remember in the Bible where there's a battle, the Holy Spirit doesn't bother talking about the clean-up after the battle — except one. This is the only place in the Bible where the Holy Spirit has chosen to highlight the clean-up after the battle. In fact, in this case, He spends the better part of the whole chapter on the subject. So it's kind of interesting to take a look at this.

First of all, we don't want to get confused about vocabulary. If the Bible talks about swords, we use that term today in its connotative, metaphorical sense. And we don't want to get hung up on horses. The Hebrew word is "souse," which means "leaper." In Jeremiah 8:7, it's translated "bird." In Exodus 14:9, it speaks of a chariot rider. It's also used of horses, but it is a leaper, whatever that is. What would Ezekiel call some of our more modern equipment? I have no idea, but souse would not be a bad choice.

In Ezekiel 39:3, God says, "I will smite thy bow out of thy left hand, and will cause thine arrows to fall out of thy right hand." What do these Hebrew words mean? Well, one of them means a sharp, piercing missile. And if you were a translator for King James of England in 1611, everybody knows what a sharp, piercing missile is. It's called an arrow. What's the other one? Well, that's the thing that launches it. Obviously a bow. Our vocabulary is the result of cultural background, not precision. If you were translating Hebrew, you could justify verse 3, saying, "I will smite thy launches out of thy left hand and thy missiles out of thy right."

Verses 9 and 10: After the battle, "they that dwell in the cities of Israel shall go forth, and shall set on fire and burn the weapons, both the shields and the bucklers, the bows and the arrows, and the handstaves and the spears, and they shall burn them with fire seven years: So that they shall take no wood out of the field, neither cut down any out of the forests; for they shall burn the weapons with fire: and they shall spoil those that spoiled them, and rob those that robbed them, saith the Lord God." Interesting passage. And if you read the ancient commentators, they were all troubled by this. They say it's obviously symbolic, because nothing can burn for seven years.

Short Shelf Life

Today we smile at that. What weapons technology could provide all the energy needs of the nation of Israel for seven years? Nuclear.

A little bit about nuclear weapons: Typically, what you have in an implosion-type bomb is a collection of material a little larger than an oversized grapefruit. Most modern weapons today are built from plutonium, which happens to be a convenient byproduct of the breeder-reactor. And the plutonium that's produced by the fuel cycle of the reactors like Chernobyl turns out to have a fairly substantial amount of short-lived isotope impurities.

It turns out that it's very delicately dependent on its geometry and its geometry alters through time due to the decay of the short-lived isotopes. So if you go through the calculations, you can determine the shelf-life.

So consider that there are 29,000 Soviet warheads, many of them now on the black market. And you can buy three of these for around $150 million, which is cheap for that sort of thing. But if you are Rafsanjani of Iran, or Assad of Syria, or Quaddafi of Libya, and you purchase a nuclear weapon, you've got a problem when you buy one. Unless you have reprocessing facilities, you're faced with something that has a limited shelf life. You either use it or lose it. It's not a long-term investment.

Until not too long ago, the actual shelf life was

highly classified stuff. But U.S. Naval Institute proceedings of April 1992 provide information relevant to a discussion about Chernobyl. From that, we can pull together the information which will indicate that the Soviet production warheads have a shelf life of seven years. They are recycled for processing every six years. I think that's kind of interesting, although I don't know how Ezekiel figured that out 2,550 years ago.

The Holy Spirit doesn't stop there, but moves on to talk about the battlefield clean-up in verse 12. "And seven months shall the house of Israel be burying them, that they may cleanse the land." And in verse 14 it says, "And they shall sever out men of continual employment . . . to cleanse it." Kind of quaint Old English, "sever out men of continual employment," but what does it mean? It means that they will hire professionals. They wait seven months before entering the area. Then they send in professionals who spend seven months cleaning up the area, and what do they do? They pick up what they find, and they bury it east of the Dead Sea in a place they're going to name the Valley of Hamongog. Translated into meteorological terms, they bury it downwind.

The Holy Spirit doesn't leave it there. Notice verse 15 says that then the travelers "that pass through the land, when any seeth a man's bone, then shall he set up a sign by it, till the buriers have buried it in the Valley of Hamongog." In other words, they don't go in for seven months, they send in the professionals, who bury whatever they can find downwind for seven months. And then when someone wanders through this area, and sees a bone that the professionals have missed, they don't touch it. They put a sign by it so the professionals can come and deal with it.

You can find that procedure in verse 15 of chapter 39. You can also find it in the U.S. Army's Operators' Manual, Marking Set, Contamination for Nuclear/Biological Chemical, Technical Memorandum 3-9905-001-10, published by the Headquarters of the Department of the Army, United States Department of the Defense.

Why the emphasis on all of this? The more we study this passage, the more we know about the actual Hebrew and the actual text, and the more we know about the current intelligence reports about the Middle East, the more we become convinced that this event could happen anytime. All the players are in place. All the arrangements are set.

Because of the break-up of the Soviet Union, most of us, of course, watch Russia and the Baltics. But the thing that we want to keep an eye on from the biblical point of view is the group of five countries we call Central Asia: Kazakhstan, Turkmenistan, Tazikistan, Uzbekistan, and Torgisia. These five republics are now independent. They have three things in common. First, they're Muslim. Second, they are short of hard currency and can't feed their people. Third, they have nuclear weapons. Kazakhstan is the fourth-largest nuclear power on earth. Kazakhstan also happens to be the site of the major Soviet space facilities. So Russia is shifting all her operations up north, latitude about 62, at the busiest space port in the world. It costs them a little more in payload, but it avoids the head-on collision with Kazakhstan.

Rafsanjani has purchased some of these nuclear weapons. He's also hired 271 technicians and engineers, but all of that is really ancient history because Yeltsin has not only signed a military assistance pact with Iran, he has also undertaken the installation of nuclear plants in Iran. He is training Iranians in nuclear techniques and also constructing a nuclear research facility.

The Central Asian republics are Muslim. It doesn't take a lot of insight to realize where their sympathies will lie. And they are obviously trading what weapons they can get their hands on with their Muslim brothers.

Terror

We could make a whole study of another subject, terrorism. The bombing of the World Trade Center has broken the psychological barrier, even though it was done in a fumbling way. Fortunately, the tragedy wasn't worse. The problem is that the bombing has signaled a green light to the independent terrorists.

When we sent our Tomahawks into Baghdad, that was intended as a signal, as a message — not just to Saddam Hussein — but to all state-sponsored terrorism. But that's all very naive, because most state-sponsored terrorism employs free contract agents in the form of these terrorist groups. There are some 30 Islamic terrorist groups that compete with one another for funds. The funds typically come from Iran and some of the other Muslim countries.

What we need to understand is that today, all they have to do is smuggle into the United States something a little larger than a footlocker and they can plant a nuclear device — not in the basement, but perhaps the top floor of the World Trade Center, or somewhere else. And if that happens, we'll probably have a 30-mile radius where we won't even be able to tell what the buildings were made out of because they will have been ionized.

We've all been told that communism is dead, though most of us would question that thesis. Consider the strategic dilemma that Russia now faces. They look to the West, and they have a Germany-dominated European super-state growing out of their traditional enemies. They look to the East and they see Japan and China, traditional enemies joining forces. They really have no choice but to build their own independent power base to the south.

And they have three choices. They obviously have to join the Muslim world. One in three in Russia is Muslim already. Or they can join the moderates: Egypt, Turkey, that group. There's no real gain for them there; they've got their own problems. For lots of reasons, Russia is not attracted to the oil-rich, independent states. They're too close to the West at the moment. Their only viable strategy is to join the radicals: Iran and Syria and Libya, and that group, which lines up with Ezekiel. It is becoming clear that is the decision they've made. Washington's tried to stop this, but with no success. Fifteen of the autonomous regions have had coup d'états and are now in the hands of the ultra-right-wing-type characters.

The Religious Opening

We've all witnessed a breathtaking period of time in recent years of being able to go into Moscow and St. Petersburg and Kiev and all these towns and start local Christian churches and there's been a tremendous opening to the gospel. But the Parliament has passed a law that says all foreign missionaries and pastors have to register with the government. It's a matter of time before it shuts down. We all knew that the window was open for only a little while. And we've used that window as best we could in the time we had, but the window is clearly going to close. The good news is that a lot of churches and fellowships have been planted throughout the former Soviet Union.

Treaty Signed

It turns out that Russia's got a very embarrassing problem, because most of their missiles, while controlled from Moscow, happen to be on Ukraine soil — and the Ukrainians happen to hate the Russians. Some of these are going to be returned, apparently, but the ones that are particularly interesting are 46 of the SS24s, which are inter-continental nuclear ballistic missiles. The Ukrainians have refused to return these; in fact, it's an open secret that they are busily trying to decode the PALs, the Permissive Action Links. These are the electronic devices that control the firing and targeting of those missiles. If they can decode them, they're theirs. Right now, they're physically in place, but there's not much they can do unless they can decode the PALs and control their launch distance and direction.

These missiles are mobile ICBMs; they can be transported by rail and each one contains 10 independently targeted warheads. There are also 600 other nuclear warheads in the Ukraine. This is such a serious problem that some observers fear Russia might pre-emptively attack the Ukraine to recover these before it all gets too far out of hand.

But another problem the Russians have is that they really don't want the Islamic fundamentalists agitating in Central Asia. The last thing in the world they want is for Iran to be starting to recruit and stir up trouble in Central Asia. They have a close relationship with the Sudan, they are putting pressure on Egypt.

Iran has got all kinds of terrorists trying to unseat its government in the hopes of bringing them into the extremist camp. And the whole Middle East, of course, is a cauldron.

So the point is, Russia's problem is that they don't want Iran to agitate in Central Asia. And Iran has agreed to that; they've signed a treaty in which, in effect, Iran agrees not to tamper with Central Asia in exchange for Moscow's military assistance should they invade another country. Obviously the target would be Israel.

The more we understand what's going on there, the more it all happens to fit the whole scenario about which Ezekiel talks.

There are 60 million Muslims in Central Asia, and this whole situation is obviously very unstable. The Russian army at the moment is very demoralized, primarily because of the widespread corruption in the senior ranks.

The KGB, on the other hand, is in much better shape. The KGB has been reorganized into four groups: the Federal Agency for Government Communications/Information, the FAPSD; the Russian Foreign Intelligence Service, the SAR; the Ministry of Security of Russian Federation, the MBRF; and the Ministry of Internal Affairs, the famous MVD. But don't be confused by this shell game. The same guys are in charge; in fact, the supreme Soviet no longer has the checks and balances over its intelligence forces that it used to have.

The real word inside is that they are just waiting for the right leader. The army's waiting for the right leader to back. The backers of Yeltsin are waiting for the right concessions to make things work with the West. There seems to be an expectation that there will be a new leader in Russia. And there are already indications that there is a swing back to a highly totalitarian, non-democratic, communist regime.

What Ezekiel implies is that they're going to get sucked in. God says, "I will put hooks in thy jaws" (Ezek. 29:4). It won't be their initial idea. The Muslims have a desire to destroy Israel. It isn't the size of Israel that is the bone of contention between the Arabs and Israel, or the Muslims and Israel. It's the existence of Israel that's the issue. And any land concessions will simply encourage them and also defeat Israel's ability to respond in anything other than a nuclear response. If the size of Israel is reduced, a nuclear weapons response is even more likely because you inhibit conventional air operations.

Fire on Magog

So, the next major conflict in the Middle East of whatever kind will likely involve nuclear weapons. When the Persian Gulf conflict started, I was very apprehensive because I was fearful that they might have had nuclear weapons. And obviously, if Saddam Hussein had them he would have used them. Now they do.

Rafsanjani of Iran has lots of delivery capability. He has range from Iran all the way to Istanbul and Cairo, not just Israel, so everybody's nervous.

So the whole Middle East situation is a cauldron. If Ezekiel 38 is about to happen, the scenario would imply that the Muslims will make a move, and because of the military assistance commitments, Russia will be sucked in and invade Israel. And if that is the event that Israel has forecast, God himself is going to intervene by wiping out the invading forces. This is going to be done in such a way that there will be an earthquake felt around the world.

I happen to believe that Ezekiel 38 precedes the events talked about in Daniel 9 and referred to as the seventieth week of Daniel. The important point to recognize, though, is that there are a number of strong arguments to indicate that the Ezekiel 38 battle will occur after the rapture of the Church.

There is one disturbing verse in this passage that no one really knows exactly how to interpret. In verse 6 of chapter 39, God says, "I will send a fire on Magog," and earlier we heard there could be hailstones of fire, "and among those that dwell carelessly

in the isles: and they shall know that I am the Lord."
The word "isles" is hard to translate because it's not
used very often in the Hebrew texts. It comes from a
root that implies a remote, pleasant island. One of the
things that bothers us here is that this exchange, the
hailstones of fire on Magog, could be the biblical
description of a nuclear exchange between the United
States and the remaining Russian missiles.

Let's look a little more closely at Russia's
military capabilities. Research the typhoon submarines. Where are they? We don't know. Why don't we
know? Because they're silent. We can't find them.
Our principal deterrent is the Ohio class Trident
submarine which is 560 feet long. It's got about a 42-
foot beam and displaces about 18,000 tons. The
Soviet counterpart to that is the typhoon class submarine: 561 feet long, same length, essentially; 78 feet in
beam, it displaces 26,500 tons. It's larger than the
biggest British cruiser during World War II. But the
disturbing thing is that it also is silent. That's why
Tom Clancey initially got into all the trouble with his
book titled *Hunt for Red October.* He supposedly
revealed classified information before it was de-
classified.

Because they were facing a quiet adversary,
they spent all their R&D in non-acoustic ASW, and
the worst-kept secret around town is that if the Soviets
have succeeded in a break-through with laser technology, they can track our tridents in real time with dual
lasers. Now what does that mean? That means our
tridents are compromised in a strategic sense. The
Russians know where they are and they can hit them.

We don't know where their typhoons are.

Each typhoon-class submarine, in fact, each of the ballistic missile submarines, has 20 tubes, carrying 20 missiles. Each missile has 10 independently targeted warheads. That means each boat has the capability to hit 200 cities. And there are more than 63 of these.

When we look at Russia today, we see a country that's in shambles, desperate. We have our own problems. We have a country that's all tangled up in the Middle East and a government that's unstable. We are in more danger today than we ever have been in our history, of having a nuclear exchange of some kind. We've got major problems. And despite the rhetoric from the administration and the pabulum we get served by the controlled media, it's time to do your homework, time to be careful.

Love Story

The good news is that I believe the Church will be gone before Ezekiel 38 happens. But again we want to return to the center of all things. You and I are beneficiaries of a love story, a love story written in blood on a wooden cross 2,000 years ago. If you're not in Jesus Christ, you've got much bigger problems than the nuclear missiles in Russia.

8

The Long War against God

Henry Morris

The evolutionary model of origins and history dominates our schools and our whole society. Whether we realize it or not, we are in a war. Do we really understand the tremendous, age-long scope of this war? It didn't begin just in our generation with Rockefeller or Rothchild. As a matter of fact, this war is basically the warfare between God and the devil, and it has been going on since the very beginning of time.

On the human level, this war expresses itself in the two world views that embrace everything. One is the God-centered world view, the other is the man-centered or the creature-centered, as against the Creator-centered world view. On the practical, scientific, logical, rational level, this finally boils down to creation versus evolution. And so the warfare between creation and evolution ultimately is the war between God and Satan. And I'd like to begin with a few verses from Revelation 12 to emphasize the tremendous worldwide, age-long scope of the long war against God.

The Deceiver

In Revelation 12:7-9 we read, "There was war in heaven: Michael and his angels fought against the dragon; and the dragon fought and his angels, And prevailed not; neither was their place found any more in heaven. And the great dragon was cast out, that old serpent, called the Devil, and Satan, which deceiveth the whole world: he was cast out into the earth, and his angels were cast out with him." Did you notice that — the devil, Satan, the old serpent, the dragon who "deceives the whole world"? Satan has deceived the whole world. He is the father of lies, he is the first murderer from the beginning, and evolution is the great lie which has led multitudes astray into all sorts of fallacies, false philosophies, false religions, and evil practices.

Satan has been the ultimate deceiver. "The whole world is under the control of the evil one" (1 John 5:19;NIV). "The God of this age has blinded the minds of unbelievers, so that they cannot see the light of the gospel of the glory of Christ, who is the image of God" (2 Cor. 4:4;NIV). Satan is the god of this age; he is the deceiver of the whole world. And from the very beginning, he has been at war with God. His essential weapon is the man-centered world view, the evolutionary world view that attempts to explain all things without God. If he is going to defeat God, he must get people to believe in something other than God, and that means he has to explain the origin and the meaning of this world without God.

So there are just these two philosophies of life, these two world views: creation versus evolution. The evolutionary world view attempts to explain the origin and development and the meaning of everything in terms of continuing natural processes which are going on today. But the creationist view says you can't do that; the basic systems of nature, the basic laws of nature, and the basic structures of nature must be explained by completed, supernatural processes which are not going on today. And so one is evolution and one is creation. And you'll notice they're exclusive. Some people try to harmonize the two and say you can believe in both, that evolution is God's method of creation. But I will try to show why you can't do that. When you simply define the terms, you'll see that they are opposites to each other. One says we can explain everything by natural processes, the other says we can't. One or the other.

To show that this premise is accepted by the evolutionary establishment, let me read from a statement by Dr. Douglas Patima, who is the author of one of the many anti-creationist books that have been published in recent years. Of course, I don't agree with much of what he says, but on this point I think he's right: "Creation and evolution between them exhaust the possible explanations for the origin of living things. Organisms either appeared on the earth fully developed or they did not. If they did not, they must have developed from pre-existing species by some process of modification. If they did appear in a fully developed state, they must indeed have been created by some omnipotent intelligence."[1] One or the other. The question is, which do we believe?

I'd like to first explore the dimensions of this warfare by considering the question of which one is valid. I think we can do this by a series of tests. One I would call the truth test: Which fits the facts of science best? Another, the fruit test: Which produces the best fruits? And the other, the biblical test: What does God say about it?

More Scientific

Insofar as the truth test is concerned, I know that we are consistently told that these creationists don't know what they're talking about. Creation is a religious view; evolution is science. So we can only teach evolution in the schools because it's scientific and creation is religion, and you can't have religion in the schools.

But the fact is that creation is far more scientific than evolution. As a matter of fact, we would say that there is not one single fact of science, real science, that supports the evolutionary philosophy whatsoever. We've had about 400 debates with leading evolutionists, and if there were any good evidences from science for evolution, we would have heard it by now. As far as we are concerned, there is none. There is no evidence of a scientific nature for evolution.

Let me illustrate by saying there is no evidence in the present or the past or the possible processes of nature to support evolution. As far as the present is concerned, who has ever seen evolution take place? Remember that science means knowledge; it's what we know, what we can observe. And who has ever observed evolution? Nobody. In all human history, nobody has ever seen one kind of creature evolve into a new kind. There are all sorts of varieties, all sorts of horizontal variation within limits, like the different varieties of dogs and the different varieties of cats. They all come from the same ancestral cat and dog, but nothing in between. There are no dats and no cogs (sic) or anything in between the cats and the dogs. There never has been and never will be because each kind is so designed that it's going to vary within the kind, horizontally. But it can never cross to another kind, and it certainly cannot evolve into a more complex kind. Sometimes groups go downhill through mutations and deterioration and maybe extinction, but that's not evolution — that's the opposite of evolution. Kind of interesting that modern ecologists and others estimate that there is at least one species, maybe more than three species, every day becoming extinct. That means thousands of species in human history have become extinct. But in all human history, nobody has ever seen one case of evolution take place. If evolution is true, it's certainly going in the wrong direction. It isn't producing anything better.

Dr. Colin Patterson, one of the world's leading evolutionists at the British Museum of Natural History, admits this. He states, "No one has ever produced a species by mechanisms of natural selection. No one's ever gotten near to it."

Charles Darwin, 135 or so years ago, became world famous for his *Origin of the Species by Natural Selection.* Everybody thinks he solved the problem. But nobody has ever produced a new species by natural selection or by any other means, for that matter. So as far as the present is concerned, there's no evolution taking place.

Dr. Pierre Grasse of France, Europe's leading zoologist, held the chair of evolution at the great Sorbonne University of Paris for 30 years. His book, *The Evolution of Living Organisms,* says this: "Today our duty is to destroy the myth of evolution, if it's considered as a simple to understand, explained phenomenon rapidly unfolding before us."[2] We don't see evolution take place. He, as an evolutionist, believes in it. But he says it took place in the past and has stopped. He continues, "Naturalists must remember that the process of evolution is revealed only through fossil forms." So he says you've got to go to the past, to fossils.

No Transitional Forms

Fossils are remains of bones, teeth, shells, footprints, or some sort of indication of former living things that are now preserved for us in the sedimentary rocks of the crust of the earth. And the idea is that the fossil record, over millions and millions of years of earth history, will show evolution from the simple to the complex over the geological ages.

It sounds convincing, and it's the main argument for evolution — the fossil record. But when you look at the fossil record in more detail, what you see are a lot of dead things. Billions of fossils have been documented, all the way from one-celled organisms to human beings and dinosaurs. In all these billions of fossils, there is not one intermediate or transitional form from one basic kind to another kind. If evolution is true, there ought to be millions of these transitional forms. There are none.

Consider carefully a statement from Dr. Steven Stanley, one of the nation's leading paleontologists, and an evolutionist. He says, "The known fossil record fails to document a single example of . . . evolution accomplishing a major morphological transition."[3]

Steven Jay Gould, who is probably the nation's most articulate evolutionist, atheist, and Marxist, of Harvard University, says that the "higher level of evolutionary transition between basic morphological designs; gradualism has always been in trouble though it remains the official position of most western evolutionists." He says, "Smooth intermediates between . . . basic structural plans are almost impossible to construct, even in thought experiments." He can't imagine a transitional form that would work.

Somebody would say, "Well, what about archaeopteryx? Isn't that an intermediate form between the bird and the reptile?" Whenever we talk about no transitional forms in our debates, they'll come back and say, "Oh, you forgot about archaeopteryx." No, archaeopteryx is not a transitional form.

Let me read what the leading researcher on

archaeopteryx has said, Dr. Allen Feduciah. Concerning the archaeopteryx, who's supposed to be part bird and part reptile, Dr. Feduciah says, "Archaeopteryx probably cannot tell us much about the early origins of feathers and flight in true proto-birds, because archaeopteryx was, in the modern sense, a bird." Already a fully developed bird. And they have found fossils of true birds that are supposedly older than archaeopteryx, so whatever archaeopteryx might have been, he was not the ancestor of birds, because birds are older than archaeopteryx was by their standard method of dating.

They really labor trying to find transitional forms and they shouldn't have to labor. If evolution was true, there ought to be millions of them. In fact, everything ought to be in transition if evolution is true. But there are not any in the past or in the present.

Don't See It

What's the proof of evolution? Dr. Mark Ridley of Oxford University has said this: "In any case, no real evolutionist, whether gradualist or punctuationist, uses the fossil record as evidence in favor of the theory of evolution" as opposed to special creation. This is one of the many articles written against creationism. But he says you can't use the fossil record if you're going to argue against creation. Dr. Grasse says they only can find evidence for evolution in the fossil record. Which one is right? They're both right. The only way to find evidence for evolution is in the fossil record, and it isn't there, so they're both right. There's no evidence anywhere.

Evolution is walked by faith, not by sight. They believe it but they don't see it. But when we point this out, they say, "Well, you have to understand, it takes millions of years to do that. So you couldn't expect to see it in the present." So we go to the fossil record, where they claim we have millions of years. And we don't see it there either, and so they say that we have to understand "that when evolution took place, it took place in spurts, very rapidly. Something evolved into something else. And that's why you don't see any fossils preserved in the transitions."

What they're saying to us is that evolution goes too slow in the present to see it, but it went too fast in the past for us to see. You don't see it anywhere; you walk by faith and not by sight.

One of the best arguments against evolution derives from the laws of thermodynamics. The laws of thermodynamics say that everything tends to be conserved in quantity and decay in quality; it goes exactly opposite to evolution. These are the best-proved laws in science.

Dr. Brent Grecko wrote an article on the second law of thermodynamics, published in *American Laboratory,* talking about experimental science. He says, "An answer can readily be given to the question, 'Has the second law of thermodynamics ever been circumvented?' Not yet."

That's his answer.

So as far as we can see, evolution is impossible and that's why we don't see it in the present or the past — it simply couldn't be. And even if it were possible, we would maintain there's not time enough for evolution. I know we talk about millions and billions of years, but that's based on evolution, actually. Nobody knows anything about that because all the history we have goes back a few thousand years. That is, real history in terms of written records. So to get any history beyond that, you have to use some physical process and apply the principle of uniformitarianism to that process. They say the present is the key to the past, so there are certain processes that will give you ages of a million years or so.

The assumption of uniformitarianism is not a valid assumption, by the way; 2 Peter 3:3-6 says that it's not valid to say that everything has been going on in the past like it is in the present. But even if we use that assumption, there are still scores of processes which will give young ages for the earth, and only three or four that will give an old age, old enough for evolution to be even thinkable, let alone practical.

So the weight of evidence is that the earth is far too young for evolution, but even if it were trillions of years old, the second law of thermodynamics says that the longer it goes on, the worse things get. It goes downhill, not uphill. There's no evidence that evolution is possible at all. So I would say that the truth test applied to evolution shows that evolution is completely false as a world view. Yet it is the basis of every discipline that's taught in the schools, and in every facet of our society.

Consider this statement from a prominent scientist, Dr. Wolfgang Smith, a Roman Catholic. He says, "We're told automatically that evolution is an established fact. But we're never told who established it, or by what means. We're told often enough that the doctrine is founded on evidence, but we're left entirely in the dark in the crucial question of what this evidence consists." Then he says, "Yet the fact remains there exists to this day not one shred of bona fide scientific evidence in support of the thesis that macro evolutionary transformations have ever occurred."[4]

C.S. Lewis is sort of an icon of Christians, of course, a great man, and he was a theistic evolutionist for a long period of his life, but later realized that was wrong. He said this towards the end of his life: "I wish I were younger. What inclines me now to think you may be right" (he was speaking to the head of the evolution protest movement in England at this time), "in regarding evolution as the central and radical lie and the whole web of falsehood that now governs our lives is not so much your arguments against it as the fanatical and twisted attitudes of its defenders."

What about the fruit test? You know, the Lord Jesus said, "A good tree cannot bring forth evil fruit, neither can a corrupt tree bring forth good fruit" (Matt. 7:18;KJV). So we can apply the fruit test, and when you do that, you'll find that the creationist tree bears all kinds of good fruit in human life, in society, in study and in science, and the evolutionary tree always bears bad fruit. This is documented thoroughly in my book, *The Long War Against God*.[5]

A Horrible Process

Consider what evolution is; it's supposedly accomplished by natural selection, the struggle for existence, the survival of the fittest. Here's what Dr. Jacques Binot, an atheist and Nobel-prize winning biologist of France, said shortly before he died: "Natural selection is the blindest and most cruel way of evolving new species and more and more complex and refined organisms. The struggle for life and elimination of the weakest is a horrible process against which our whole modern ethics revolts." I'm surprised that any Christian would ever defend the idea that this is a process which God used in order to have evolution.

Don't think you, as a Christian, can be an evolutionist, a Christian evolutionist as I was myself, all through college. People ask, "Can't you be a Christian evolutionist?" Yes. You can be a Christian liar, you can be a Christian adulterer, you can be a Christian thief. Christians can be all kinds of things they ought not to be; but that doesn't make it right. There's no evidence for evolution, it produces bad fruit. The whole process is completely based on struggle and suffering and dying in order to produce evolutionary advances. Dr. David Hull, a professor of philosophy at Northwestern University, speaking on this says, "The evolutionary process is arrived at with happenstance, contingency, incredible waste, death, pain, and horror. Whatever the god implied by evolutionary theory may be like, he is not a loving god who cares about his productions. He is careless, wasteful, indifferent, almost diabolical. He is certainly not the sort of god to whom anyone would be inclined to pray."

If you feel like you've got to believe in evolution, then atheism is the logical implication. But don't blame God for evolution. He wouldn't do a thing like that. That's the most wasteful, inefficient, cruel process anybody could ever think of with which to produce man.

Evolution is the basis of atheism, the basis of humanism. The American Humanist Association, formed by John Dewey and others back in 1933, and the *Humanist Magazine*, and the Humanist Manifesto all came out about the same time by the same group of people. The various tenets of the Humanist Manifesto, the very first one, were that, "We believe that the universe was not created; it evolved." And the second one, "We believe that man was not created; man evolved." And everything else follows from that premise. The whole system of secular humanism is based on evolution, even evolutionary theistic humanism.

Leading Writers

Julian Huxley, the first director general of UNESCO, published a white paper to guide UNESCO in its formative years. He states, "We must develop a world religion of evolutionary humanism." This was the primary goal set for his leadership in UNESCO.

Julian Huxley was the leading evolutionist of the twentieth century until he died a few years ago. He was the person most responsible for the system known as neo-Darwinism and he wrote many, many books. He was also the great convocation speaker at the centennial convocation for the University of Chicago commemorating the hundredth anniversary of Charles Darwin's book in 1959. A passionate evolutionist, his whole system was based on evolutionary humanism. He acknowledged that these beliefs constituted a religion, and he even wrote a book, *Religion Without Revelation,* setting forth that philosophy.

More recently we look at Isaac Asimov, who was the president of the American Humanist Association when he died just a couple of years ago. Isaac Asimov was probably the most prolific science writer to ever live. He wrote about 500 books and innumerable articles about every imaginable thing in science. If anybody knew science, he did. But he was an atheist. He said, "I'm an atheist, out and out. Emotionally, I'm an atheist. I don't have the evidence to prove that God doesn't exist, but I so strongly suspect He doesn't, I don't want to waste my time."[6] But notice what he says: "I don't have the evidence to prove that there is no God." And he knew science better than most anyone else. So if he didn't have evidence to prove that there is no God, nobody does. Atheism is not based on science.

That was also Charles Darwin's basic problem. He didn't want to believe in the God of the Bible and he didn't want to believe in Christianity, and so he tried to find a way to get away from it.

Other Fruits

There are other fruits of the evolutionary tree besides humanism and atheism. There is also, for example, racism. The title of Charles Darwin's book was *The Origin of the Species by Natural Selection,* and the subtitle was, *The Preservation of Favored Races in the Struggle for Life.* In his 1874 book, *The Descent of Man,* he says, "At some future period, the civilized races of man will almost certainly exterminate and replace the savage races throughout the world." This is all a natural development of evolution and the survival of the fittest. In the process of evolution, of course, the races are in an ascending order of evolutionary development with the Caucasian race at the top, the Negro race at the bottom, and these savage races are going to be exterminated in the struggle for existence.

Thomas Huxley, who was the most notorious evolutionary speaker of the nineteenth century, said, "No rational man cognizant of the facts can believe that the average Negro is the equal, still less the superior of the white man." Now, this is not some southern fundamentalist bigot saying things like this. These are the leading evolutionists of the century. Furthermore, racism among evolutionary anthropologists persisted up until World War II and practically all the American anthropologists were racists.

Henry Fairfield Osborn, head of the American Museum of Natural History, published an article in the *Humanist Magazine* in which he said "The average Negro has the intelligence of a 12-year-old boy of the species Homo sapiens."[7] In other words, the Negro is not even a member of the same species, according to him.

Now, understand that no evolutionist says that today. Modern evolutionists don't believe that. They're not racists today because Hitler gave racism a bad name with his genocidal projects in World War II. But the roots of racism, the rationale for racism, is the struggle for existence, not only among animals, but among people and races, classes.

Karl Marx, of course, based his whole system, class struggle, on evolution. He wanted to dedicate his book, *Das Kapital*, to Charles Darwin. All the evolutionists and the Communists of the last two centuries — Marx, Engels, Lenin, Stalin, and others — were strong evolutionists. You had to be an evolutionist to be a Communist. All the Socialists were, and the Nazis were, and the Fascists were.

Let me quote what Daniel Gasman, in his book *The Scientific Origins of National Socialism,* says: "Hitler stressed and singled out the idea of biological evolution as the most forceful weapon against traditional religion, and he repeatedly condemned Christianity for its opposition to the teachings of evolution. For Hitler, evolution was the hallmark of modern science and culture."[8] Bad fruits from bad roots.

We don't need to infer that capitalism is inherently any better. Many do not realize that the laissez-faire capitalism of the nineteenth century was also based on Darwinian evolution. We read in a recently published book by James Rachels, professor of philosophy at the University of Alabama-Birmingham: "The survival of the fittest was quickly interpreted as an ethical precept that sanctioned cutthroat, economic competition. Capitalist giants such as John D. Rockefeller and Andrew Carnegie regularly invoked what they took to be Darwinian principles to explain the ethics of the American system. Rockefeller, in a talk to his Sunday school class, proclaimed that 'the growth of large business is merely survival of the fittest. The American Beauty rose can be produced, and the splendor and fragrance brings cheer to its beholder only by sacrificing the early buds which grew up around it. This isn't an evil tendency in business, it's merely the working out of the law of nature, and the law of God.' "[9]

Andrew Carnegie said, "While this law may sometimes be hard for the individual, it's best for the race because it ensures the survival of the fittest in every department."

Mr. Carnegie said in his autobiography that evolution came in like a light, because it not only eliminated the need for God, but it justified him in his business practices.[10]

Common Aspects

There is much concern today about the New Age movement, and that also is based on evolution. From witchcraft, astrology, and spiritism on the one hand and morphogenetic fields, the anthropic principle, and networking on the other hand, all kinds of different systems go into the New Age movement. But all of them have two things in common. One is that they're all based on evolution as the beginning, as the background. The other is that they all have the goal of globalism, or world culture with a world religion and a world government. I think you'll find this to be true without exception.

Several years ago, Marilyn Ferguson, the author of *The Aquarian Conspiracy*, which is sort of a bible of the New Age movement, surveyed the leading dealers of the different New Age movements. She asked who their spiritual guru was, the one who most influenced them in their thinking. By far the majority pointed to the Jesuit priest/paleethnologist, Teilhard de Chardin.[11]

Here's what de Chardin says in his book, *The Phenomenon of Man:* "Is evolution a theory, a system, a hypothesis? It's much more. It's a general condition to which all theories, all systems, all hypotheses must bow, and which they must satisfy henceforward if they are to be thinkable and true. Evolution is the light which illuminates all fact, the curve that all lines of thought must follow."[12]

He might just as well have put "god" in place of "evolution" there. Evolution was his god. And, of course, the goal was what he called the Omega Point and the ultimate world culture and world religion. We would all be submerged in this great unity of philosophy.

You might say, "Well, yes, but wasn't he a Christian? Didn't he believe in Jesus Christ, since he was a priest?" In another book, one that was written not long before he died, he says, "It is Christ in very truth who saves. But then we must immediately add that at the same time it is Christ who is saved by evolution."[13] Evolution was his god, and he's the leading light of the New Age movement.

Robert Miller, who is also a leading light in the present New Age movement and former assistant secretary general of the United Nations, said, "I believe the most fundamental thing we can do today is to believe in evolution. So I hope you begin to see how evolution is not merely a peripheral matter that we don't need to be much concerned about; it's basic in everything."

We fight all these bad fruits. We fight communism, socialism, pornography, and abortion and all that. But we're trying to cut out the fruits, which is leaving the roots, and the fruits are going to grow back. To get the weeds out of the garden, you've got to get the seeds out of the ground. And the root of all this is the evolutionary world view, which has been dominating the world since the very beginning.

I mentioned abortion. We get all concerned, and we ought to, about the Right To Life movement. But the reason people think that abortion is okay is because they don't believe that this fetus, as they call it, is really a human being yet. Well, where do they get that idea? They get that idea from evolution. Do you know that one of the most cogent ideas of the nineteenth century was the idea of the continuity of being, the great chain of being, that there's a continuity of life at all levels, from the highest to the lowest.

The idea was that, in the development of the embryo, it had to go through all the stages, all the various forms of being. It started out as a one-celled organism in the liquid environment, then it grew to a multi-celled invertebrate, and it finally became a fish with gills and slits, and then an amphibian and a reptile, and finally a monkey with a tail and eventually a human being. That's the so-called law of ontogeny recapitulates phylogeny. You remember that, maybe, from high school. That theory was disproved long ago. It really isn't true at all. An embryo never does go through a fish stage with gills, it never has a tail like a monkey or anything like that. It's been completely disproved scientifically, and most modern biologists reject it. But it's still taught in high schools quite a bit, and we've encountered it in our debates, too.

Let's look at what is really behind the abortion issue. This is from an article by Ilie A. Schneour, who was director of the Biosystems Research Institute in Lahoya, California. He said, "Ontogeny recapitulates phylogeny. This is the fundamental tenet of modern biology that derives from the evolutionary theory and is thus anathema to creationism as well as those opposed to freedom of choice. Ontogeny is the name for the process of development of a fertilized egg into a fully-formed and mature living organism. Phylogeny, on the other hand, is the history of the evolution of a species, in this case the human being. During development, the fertilized egg progresses over 38 weeks to what is in fact a rapid passage through evolutionary history from a single primordial cell. The concept progresses through being something of a protozoa and a fish, a reptile, a bird, a primate, ultimately a human being."[14]

And you see, if you kill this creature, it's no great thing to kill a fish or a monkey; it's not a human being yet. And the scientific rationale for abortion is this recapitulation theory that the embryo is going through evolution and isn't human yet.

Now, not every woman who has an abortion, or doctor who performs one, is an evolutionist. People

commit sin for all kinds of reasons. But when proponents try to give a scientific rationale for it, they have
to go back to evolution again. Carl Sagan has written
about this same sort of thing, as well as others. I
believe you can show that evolution is at the root of
our drug culture, our pornographic influence, our
basic immorality approach to life today and so on.
Evil fruits, without exception, based on the evolutionary roots.

The Bible Says . . . What?

What about the biblical test? Well, of course,
the Bible gives no countenance for evolution at all.
Ten times in the first chapter of Genesis God states,
"after its kind." Fruit trees produce fruit trees after
their kind, creeping things after their kind, man after
mankind.

And when we look at this matter of race:
There's only one race biblically, that's the human
race. Never has an ape become a man, never has any
kind of organism evolved into a different kind. The
Bible is clear on that; it gives no countenance for
evolution whatsoever.

Furthermore, the Bible says that whatever
God was doing in creating and making everything, as
given in the first chapter of Genesis, He stopped
doing. The heavens and the earth were finished, all the
host of them. On the seventh day, God ended His work
which He had made. He rested on the seventh day
from all His work which He had made, and He blessed
the seventh day, sanctified it, because in it He rested
from all of His work which He created and made.

We can never determine anything about the development of life through the study of present processes, like the evolutionists want to believe. We can't do it because God stopped doing those processes of creation and now the basic law is conservation and decay, the first and second laws of thermodynamics. He is conserving what He created; the Bible says that. He's upholding all things by the power of His Word. He's not creating anything because He stopped creating at the end of the six days, except in occasional miracles.

Six Days

I don't want to be offensive, but I believe the Bible is very plain that the creation took place in six literal days, several thousand years ago. We don't need to impose the evolutionary system of billions of years of geological history. After all, these geological ages are based on the fossil record, and fossils are dead things that suffered and died before they were buried. And that means if all this took place before man was created and before man sinned, then God is responsible for instituting a whole system of billions of animals suffering and dying in the course of evolution for no reason, if man is the goal of all this.

The Bible says by one man sin entered in the world, and death by sin. First Corinthians 15 says, "By man came death." And if somebody says, "Well, that just means human death," the answer is no. Romans 8:22 says, "We know that the whole creation has been groaning as in the pains of childbirth right up to the present time" (NIV). Jesus Christ himself, remember, said in Mark 10:6, "From the beginning of the creation God made them male and female." He is quoting from Genesis 1 and the creation of Adam and Eve. He said that God made them male and female, not by a billion years after the beginning of the creation, but from the beginning of the creation. Right from the very beginning, God's purpose was to create and redeem man. There would be no purpose in billions of years of animals living and dying and becoming extinct. The Bible does not allow for any concession to evolution whatever.

In a book called, *Biblical Creationism* I've examined every single verse in the whole Bible that deals with creation or the Flood or anything similar.[15] The whole Bible teaches very plainly that God made everything in the whole universe in six days several thousand years ago. To come away with any other concept, you've got to read it into it, not out of it.

In the context of the Bible, God defines His terms, and in Genesis 1:5-6 it says that God, "separated the light from the darkness. God called the light "day," and the darkness he called "night." And there was evening, and there was morning — the first day" (NIV). The first day was just like every other day: Evening and morning, light and darkness, 24 hours, essentially. God defined it that way.

"Remember the Sabbath day by keeping it holy. Six days you shall labour and do all your work, but the seventh day . . . you shall not do any work. . . . For in six days the Lord made the heavens and the earth, the sea, and all that is in them, but he rested on the seventh day" (Exod. 20:8-11;NIV). Same words, same construction. If they're not the same kinds of days, then God can't communicate. He wrote this down with His own finger on a tablet of stone. All Scriptures are divinely inspired, but this part was divinely inscribed. God wrote it down himself, and communicated very plainly that He made everything in six days. The reason we keep time in weeks is because God did, and it's been that way ever since the beginning.

Founding Fathers Were Creationists

The Bible test, of course, does not support evolution. There's not a hint of evolution anywhere in the Bible. The creationist world view, on the other hand, fits all the facts of science. These gaps between the kinds are exactly what we predict from creation. We predict there would be no transitional forms in the fossil record, and sure enough, there are none. We predict the laws of thermodynamics. We predict that everything is now being conserved — that's the first law — because He is now upholding all things by the power of His Word. We predict He's not creating anything, having rested from all of His work. It says in Hebrews 4:3 that all of God's "works were finished from the foundation of the world" (KJV). And so on. Everything that we see in the real world of real science supports the creation record of the Bible.

That is why the founding fathers of science were creationists. Isaac Newton; Johann Kepler, the father of astronomy; Robert Boyle, the father of chemistry, Maxwell; Faraday; or Pasteur, and many of the great founding fathers of science were Bible-believing Christian creationists.

And so creation produces good fruits. It's the basis of true science. It's the basis of true education. It's the basis, in fact, of true Americanism.

Have you ever stopped to think about that? There are arguments about Jefferson not being a Christian, and Franklin and Thomas Payne, but the basic structure of our government was based on biblical law. Let me put before you a statement from Gilman Ostrander, a historian of science. He said, "The American nation was founded by intellectuals who accepted a world view based on biblical authority as well as Newtonian science. They assume that God created the earth and all life on it at the time of creation, and continued without change thereafter. Adam and Eve were God's final creations and all mankind had descended from them. When Thomas Jefferson, in his old age, was confronted with the newly developing science of geology, he rejected the evolutionary concept of the creation of the earth on the grounds that no all-wise and all-powerful creator would have gone about the job in such a slow, inefficient way." No one has answered that question.

Jefferson may not have been a fundamentalist Christian like we would define it today, but he was a creationist, and so were Thomas Payne, and Ben Franklin. They believed in God, who had created all things in the beginning. They were creationists, and so, "all men are created equal. . . . We've been endowed by our Creator with certain inalienable rights," from the Declaration of Independence. And our whole system of American constitutional government was based on the premise that there is a God who created this world and who governs it, and we are responsible to Him.

We could continue examining fruits — education and psychology and economics. True economics, psychology and education are rooted in creation, but the way they're taught today is based on evolution.

And most importantly, true Christianity is based on creation. Many have argued, "That's all right if you want to believe in creation. Don't make an issue of it. You just need to get people saved. Just preach the gospel. Preach Christ. Don't preach creation, that's controversial and you don't need to do that."

Oh, yes you do. Because true Christianity and every real Christian doctrine is founded squarely upon the doctrine of special creation in the beginning.

Let's consider a couple of Scriptures that bear this out. Just preach Christ? Absolutely. You know the greatest Christological passage in the Bible probably is Colossians 1:16-17: "For by him all things were created: things in heaven and on earth, visible and invisible, whether thrones or powers or rulers or authorities; all things were created by him and for him. He is before all things, and in him all things hold together" (KJV). John says, "In the beginning was the Word, and the Word was with God, and the Word was God. The same was in the beginning with God. All things were made by him; and without him was not any thing made that was made" (John 1:1-3;KJV).

Jesus Christ is the Creator. You can't preach Christ as He really is without preaching Him as the

Creator. And the reason we need Him as Saviour and Redeemer is because we rebelled against Him as our Creator. That's basically what sin is. The real Jesus Christ was our Creator and He became our Saviour. He's our coming King and Lord. So what is this gospel that we are supposed to preach?

I like to make word studies in the Bible, and it turns out that there are 101 references to the gospel in the New Testament. Very nice symmetrical pattern. The middle one, 50 before and 50 after, is 1 Corinthians 15:1-3, where Paul says, "Moreover, brethren, I declare unto you the gospel which I preached unto you, which also ye have received, and wherein ye stand; By which also ye are saved, if ye keep in memory what I preached unto you, unless ye have believed in vain. for I delivered unto you first of all that which I also received, how that Christ died for our sins according to the scriptures" (KJV). So Paul says the central focus of the gospel is the substitutionary death and burial and resurrection of Jesus Christ for our sins. That's the focus of the gospel.

Remember there are 100 others, though. When we look at those we find an interesting pattern. The very first time the word "gospel" is used is in Matthew 4:23 where it says, "Jesus Christ went about all Galilee, teaching in their synagogues, and preaching the gospel of the kingdom." So from the very beginning He was preaching a gospel which included a coming Kingdom when He would be acknowledged by all of His creatures as King of kings and Lord of lords. Every knee would bow and every tongue would confess that He was Lord.

The last time the word is used is in Revelation 14:6-7, where John says, "I saw another angel fly in the midst of heaven, having the everlasting gospel to preach unto them that dwell on the earth ... saying ... Fear God, and give glory to him; for the hour of his judgment is come: and worship him that made heaven, and earth, and the sea, and the fountains of waters."

What is this everlasting gospel? "Worship him who made heaven and earth and the sea and the fountains of waters." Since it's everlasting, it can never change. Paul, as you remember, said in Galatians 1:8, if even "an angel from heaven, preach any other gospel unto you than that which we have preached unto you, let him be accursed" (KJV). And here's an angel from heaven preaching a gospel that includes the gospel of creation.

I like to put it this way: A gospel without the creation has no foundation. The gospel without the coming Kingdom has no hope. The gospel without the Cross and the empty tomb has no power. But if you have the complete gospel — past, present, and future — a sure foundation of blessed hope and all power in heaven and earth, that's the gospel we're to preach to every creature. We can't really preach the gospel without creation as its foundation. Every basic doctrine of Christianity is founded squarely upon creation. It's not an incidental matter; it's basic to everything.

The Race for Evolution

Where did this all come from? What's the historical basis of this conflict, this age-long war? It didn't begin with Charles Darwin. A lot of people thought Darwin began evolution but evolution was around a long time before Darwin. He didn't even invent the theory of natural selection. In my research for the book, *The Long War Against God,* I found that there were at least 11 other men who published papers on natural selection before Darwin did. In fact, it's kind of interesting that the co-discoverer of natural selection was believed to be Alfred Russell Wallace, who developed the idea at the same time that Darwin did.

The conditions under which that discovery was made were very interesting. At the time that Darwin's evolutionism was becoming accepted, back in England, ancient spiritism was being revived which promulgated the modern ideas of channeling that are so prominent in the New Age movement. Alfred Russell Wallace was a leader in this spiritist movement in England and he wrote books on the subject. He was also a very careful scientist; he wrote books on economics and other subjects. However, it's interesting that he had no education, he was completely self-trained.

Darwin had been educated. He didn't do very well, but he went to Oxford and Cambridge and got a degree in theology. After that, he worked in London with all the leading scientists of the day, and he continued developing his theory of natural selection over a period of 20 years, working back and forth with the leading scientists of England at the time. But he was afraid to publish his theory because he didn't think he had enough evidence yet.

Then all of a sudden, Wallace addressed a letter to him saying that he had this idea of how species originated. It turned out to be exactly the same as Darwin's theory, and Darwin was so afraid that Wallace was going to get priority that he rushed his book into print. His book, *Origin of the Species,* probably never would have been printed at all had it not been for Wallace challenging him on priority.

In his autobiography, Alfred Russell Wallace explains how this idea of natural selection came to him. While he was prominent in the spiritist movement, he'd also spent much of his life in the South American jungles and in the jungles of Malaysia. There he worked with so-called primitive people who were animists and who worshipped the spirits and believed that they could communicate with the spirits. That was very consistent with what Wallace believed in England.

He states, "I was then," [that is, in February 1858] "living in the Moluccas and was suffering from a rather severe attack of intermittent fever which prostrated me every day during the cold and succeeding hot fits. During one of these fits while again considering the problem of the origin of the species, something led me to think of Malthus' essay on population. Then the whole method of species modification became clear to me, and in the two hours of my fit, I had thought out all the main points of the theory. That same evening, I sketched out the draft of the paper, and in the two succeeding evenings I wrote it out and sent it by the next post to Mr. Darwin."[16]

It's very interesting that in two hours of a fit in the midst of a jungle, Wallace came up with the same theory that Darwin had been developing in the midst of a scientific community for 20 years.

Here's what Loren Eiseley, great historian of science at the University of Pennsylvania, said in his article on Wallace: "A man pursuing birds of paradise in a remote jungle did not yet know that he had forced the world's most reluctant author to discharge his hoarded volume. Or that the whole of western thought was about to be swung into a new channel because a man in a fever felt a moment of a strange radiance."[17] Make what you want to out of that.

Richard Wurmbrand, in his book, *Marx and Satan*, has shown that Karl Marx was not an atheist as many people believe, but a Satanist.[18]

Dr. Paul Vitts, in his treatment of Sigmund Freud, shows that there's a very strong likelihood that Freud made a pact with the devil. And all these leaders of evolutionary thought of the nineteenth and early twentieth centuries seemed to have been more involved than just scientists. I believe these are indications that we're in a war not with flesh and blood but against spiritual wickedness in the heavenly places against the principalities and powers of darkness. That's the real secret.

We know further that this evolutionary philosophy was sort of underground during the Middle Ages, but it was blossoming in full fruit during the

period of Greek and Roman philosophy. The Epicureans and the stoics whom Paul encountered were
evolutionists. If you read their philosophy, you recognize that they are very similar to modern evolutionists. The stoics were pantheistic evolutionists; the
Epicureans were atheistic evolutionists, much like
our modern division between the two schools of
evolutionary thought. We can trace that back through
Plato and finally back to the Moluccan school back in
Malthus, and they believed, of course, in evolution.
They were atheists.

So there were these two schools of thought:
pantheistic evolution — that everything was God, and
atheism — that nothing was God. But of course
they're really the same thing because if God is everywhere in general then He's nowhere in particular. And
all of them rejected the idea of a real creation and a real
creator. They were all evolutionists, all the ancient
philosophers and all the ethnic religions both ancient
and modern — the Greeks, the Romans, the
Confucionists, the Hindus, the Buddhists and so forth.
These are pantheistic evolutionists and all of them
reject the idea of creation. And everywhere you look,
the evolutionary tree produces fruits that are harmful
in philosophy and harmful in practice.

Babylon — the Beginning

If we go back far enough, we see that this
evolutionary philosophy ultimately had its origin
in ancient mythology. Peter and Paul refer to this.
Paul says, "Beware lest any man spoil you through
philosophy and vain deceit, after the tradition of

men . . . not after Christ" (Col. 2:8;KJV). And Peter says, "We have not followed cunningly devised fables" (2 Pet. 1:16).

It's interesting that these myths all trace their origin back to Babylon. The ancient Sumarians believed in evolution, which brings us back to the Bible and the time of Nimrod and the Tower of Babel when they wanted to make a name for themselves and dedicate a great tower unto the heavens, the host of heavens. There was a great shrine at the top of the Tower of Babel, and God confused their tongues and scattered them. They couldn't speak to each other anymore, but they carried the same religion with them everywhere.

So the same basic system of gods and goddesses, pantheism, polytheism, idolatry, spiritism, and astrology all over the world comes from that original source in Babylon. That's why the Bible calls Babylon the "mother of harlots and abominations of the earth." (Rev. 17:5). That's where it began.

And where did Nimrod get the idea? I believe he got it from Satan, from the host of heaven that he was trying to worship. Satan is the deceiver of the whole world. He's the father of liars. Was Satan the first evolutionist? Remember his proposition to Adam and Eve — "You will be like God" (Gen. 3:5;NIV). Humanism: God is not really the Creator; you can be just like Him.

Who Will Win?

Satan is still trying to defeat God. He didn't believe the Word of God, and that's the basic root of every sin: rejecting God's Word. God told him He had created him, but Satan refused to believe it. And so he said, "Well, I can be like God" (see Isa. 14:14).

We are in a warfare, and it's not a warfare with men and women and systems and philosophies and governments. It's spiritual warfare, and it's got to be fought in spiritual terms. We're not going to win by bullets or by ballots. We are going to win, though. In 2 Corinthians 10:3-5, it says that "We walk in the flesh, we do not war after the flesh. (For the weapons of our warfare are not carnal, but mighty through God to the pulling down of strongholds;) Casting down imaginations, and every high thing that exalteth itself against the knowledge of God, and bringing into captivity every thought to the obedience of Christ."

We have to "put on the whole armour of God" (Eph. 6:11), for we are to have our loins girded about with truth and we have on the breastplate of righteousness and the helmet of salvation and the shoes of the gospel of peace, and the shield of faith and the sword of the spirit and always in the spirit of prayer. We wrestle not against flesh and blood.

But we are going to win. Paul says, "Evil men and seducers shall wax worse and worse. . . . But continue thou in the things which thou hast learned. . . . All scripture is given by inspiration of God, and is profitable" (2 Tim. 3:13-16). I charge thee therefore before God. . . . Preach the word; be instant in season, out of season (2 Tim. 4:1-2;KJV).

Stick close to the Word. Jesus said, "Occupy 'til I come" (Luke 19:13). We know that in the last days the world will see this great humanistic beast, this great man of sin who's going to finally get all the world under his domain for a little while. All the kings of the earth are going to give their allegiance to him. They're going to worship him; they're going to worship the dragon who gave his power to the beast. Everyone will be a Satan worshipper in that day except those whose names are written in the Lamb's Book of Life. And it says, "These shall make war with the Lamb, and the Lamb shall overcome them: for he is Lord of lords, and King of kings: and they that are with him are called, and chosen, and faithful" (Rev. 17:14;KJV).

So let us be found faithful.

9

Is America Moving toward Socialism?

Don McAlvany

If there is one way to describe the time we live in today, it is that we live in a great time of deception, I believe perhaps the greatest time of deception in all of world history. The deception permeates every aspect of our lives: television, radio, newspapers, magazines, books — just about everywhere we turn. It's my prayer that you can learn how to discern the truth while living in a purposefully deceptive environment.

Despite the deception, these are exciting times in which we live. In fact, I think that these are the most exciting times in all of history. We are going to see things in the next five to seven years that none of us have ever seen before. We are going into a period of challenge, pressure, and difficulty, unlike anything that has ever happened in the history of the United States, perhaps in the history of the world. I believe we're soon going to lose most of our freedom in this country — unless we make some major changes. I believe that we are seeing the forces of darkness gather. I believe these are the times that could herald the return of our Lord Jesus Christ to the earth as King. But, regardless of the exact nature and events, the near future *will* be exciting.

Deception All Around Us

Americans are perpetual optimists; we like good news, we don't like bad news. We don't like people who bring us bad news. This is called by psychologists "the Pollyanna Principle." "Tell me what I want to know or don't tell me anything at all." The American people don't want to be moved out of their comfort zone. They're very comfortable.

Francis Schaeffer said that the 1990s would be a time when most people, especially Christians, would be interested in one thing: peace and personal affluence. "Leave me alone, give me peace, let me do my own thing." Therefore, we have a group of people in this country who are very, very optimistic. I believe with all my heart that optimism will be shattered in the not too distant future.

To win in the battle for investment return, politics, business, or whatever, you have to avoid being an optimist or a pessimist, but be a realist. You must look at things the way they actually are. The same goes for watching world events, you must have a clear perspective.

Complacency is self-satisfaction accompanied by unawareness of actual dangers or deficiencies. There is a tremendous amount of complacency in our country today. Complacency and apathy on the part of Christians is very dangerous. We've had about 50 years of uninterrupted prosperity. This has caused the American people in general, and Christians in particular, to become fat, dumb, lazy, and very complacent. There seem to be people in our country who would like to destroy our freedom, our Constitution, our traditional way of life, all in the name of a better world. If Americans don't wake up and defend what God has entrusted to them, I think the prognosis for our country is poor.

I think you have to look beyond what the politicians are telling you and what you're seeing on television if you want to know what's really going on today. Jesus said in Matthew 24:4, "Watch out that no one deceives you" (NIV). He talks about a time of great deception prior to His return, and I think we are living in that time of great deception. Second Thessalonians 2:3 says, "Don't let anyone deceive you in any way, for that day will not come until the rebellion occurs" (NIV). We live in a day of rebellion.

I believe we live in the greatest day and era of deception in all of world history right now. What comes into our brain, through the liberal media, is very carefully controlled. Controlled in the way they shape the thoughts and opinions of the masses to fit the "world view" mold.

Many things that are happening today are not

as they appear. They are not what your television is showing you, what your politicians are claiming, or what your newspaper says. If the media doesn't want you to believe something, it will discredit it — even factual arguments or truth. The media does this by attacking and discrediting, and it works. In Latin, this is called, *argumentum ad hominem*, or "argument against the man." Properly manipulated, a person can be neutralized, and no one will listen to what he has to say. You can find Christians and conservatives all over this country who have been tarred and feathered by the political left — all because they told the truth.

Few events are spontaneous or accidental, and many are manipulated. Unless you accept that fact, you'll always have a hard time understanding what's going on in the world. There are powerful forces behind the scenes, pulling the strings on the Bill and Hillary Clintons, and on most events that we see happening around the world.

Most politicians and government authorities will lie, without hesitation, to protect their own interests. I know that doesn't come as a surprise to most of you. I primarily spend my time analyzing and speaking in the area of economic systems. It's interesting to observe each presidential administration as they continually lie about the state of the U.S. economy, the money supply, unemployment, productivity, etc.

Machiavelli said in his book, *The Prince*, that governments are constituted to lie to the greatest number of people the greatest amount of time. So ignore what the politicians say, but watch closely what they do. What they do is much more important than what they say.

The 1990s will witness a tremendous loss of freedom. There's no group of people in this country that should be more concerned about freedom than Christians because, if we lose our freedom, we're going to lose the freedom to preach the gospel of Jesus Christ.

Throughout history, the bearer of bad news has been unpopular. In the ancient world, such people were stoned — they literally threw stones at them. It was called the "shoot the messenger syndrome."

Hosea 4:6 says, "My people are destroyed from lack of knowledge" (NIV). I think as we lose our freedom in this country it will be largely because our people are not receiving the knowledge to make good decisions. Americans have forgotten the greatness in our Constitution, the importance of our Christian heritage, the uniqueness of our position in Christ, and our biblical charge to take a stand against evil. If we do lose our freedom, it will be from lack of knowledge.

I constantly plead with people to get out of debt and spread their assets into several investments. But a lot of Christians come to me and say, "If you trusted God, you wouldn't think of such things, you would simply sit down and pray." Well, I do like to sit down and pray, and I do trust God, but the Bible does say in Proverbs 27:12, "The prudent see danger and take refuge, but the simple keep going and suffer for it" (NIV). I am now convinced that there's a lot more simple than there are prudent.

The Decline of the United States

• *Monetary and Economic Decline*

This is based on the false premise that man can have or create something out of nothing, and we've seen our government run the printing presses for decades now and create a tremendous amount of inflation.

We have seen the biggest debt pyramid explosion in the history of the United States in the last 15 to 20 years, with most of it happening under the Republicans. We went from George Washington through Jimmy Carter, 206 years, from zero to $3 trillion in total debt — corporate, private, and governmental. And in 13 more years, we went from $3 trillion to $16 trillion, a 550 percent increase in 13 years over what it took in the previous 206 years. That debt pyramid is now coming unglued, and many financial experts are worried we're headed for a major depression.

We had a million Americans go bankrupt last year, including a lot of Christians who ignored what the Bible has to say about debt. We had over 100,000 corporations go down last year. We've had several thousand banks and savings and loans close in recent years. We're moving into some very, very difficult times. I think there are some constructive things that you can do if you want to try to protect your assets during this impending economic decline. Especially if, like many believe, it accelerates dramatically.

• *Social and Political Decline*

The government is trying hard to redistribute wealth based on the false premise that all men are equal, can be made equal through redistribution of wealth, or through government edict. They may occasionally take a step backward before moving forward again, but the socialization of America is well entrenched. The great lie of the French Revolution was "Liberty, Equality, Fraternity." What were we told by the socialists of that day was that everyone was equal. (Of course, some of the socialists were more equal than others, but that was okay from their viewpoint.) To make everybody equal they take from the rich, the earners, the workers, the producers, and give to the poor and the non-producers. They also put controls on the "greedy" business people who can't be left alone to control themselves. That is basic socialism.

I believe that America is plunging toward socialism. We are seeing more socialistic legislation and controls over every aspect of the American people's lives coming down the pike than we've ever seen in the history of this country, and it has accelerated rapidly since Bill and Hillary Clinton were elected to the White House.

The Clinton co-presidency may be like our worst nightmare coming true. It has been estimated that over one million people have seen *The Clinton Chronicles* video, connecting Clinton directly to drugs, sex, murder, and lies. It will open your eyes as to who gets elected president in the U.S.

Clinton wanted socialized medicine, homosexuals in the military, disarmament, and dismantling of the U.S. military. Bill Clinton campaigned for McGovern shortly after he came back from his anti-war activities in London and Moscow in 1970. It's estimated that he spent about two weeks on the tab or hosted by the KGB back in 1970 while our boys were fighting and dying in Vietnam.

Most of the top echelon of the Clinton administration are members of the Council on Foreign Relations and/or the Tri-Lateral Commission. The top 35 members of the administration, including the entire cabinet, belong to the CFR, the Tri-Lateral Commission, or one of the leftist institutes: International Economics or Policy Studies. There were over 10 open homosexuals on the Clinton transition team. The Clinton administration is far and away the most left-wing administration in U.S. history. The same people who gave away the Panama Canal and opened the door to massive KGB, GRU, and DGI penetration of the U.S. in the Carter administration now dominate Clinton's administration. America now has the most dangerous foreign policy team and domestic policy team in U.S. history.

I personally believe that Bill and Hillary are actually low-ranking employees of the behind-the-scenes powers, as expendable as Jimmy Carter or George Bush. Many people, myself included, believe that America is controlled by a small group of people, maybe even going back as far as the Illuminati. It started in 1776 as a group of Satan worshippers. The story goes that they became very wealthy in Europe and decided they needed to control the world's central banks and financial systems. This would eventually bring about world government that their ultimate leader, Satan, could use to manage the whole world. Whether it's the Illuminati, or the Tri-Lateral Commission, the Council on Foreign Relations, the Bilderburgers, the Club of Rome, the Socialist International, the Fabian Socialists, or other globalistic-oriented groups, they all openly want world government by the year 2000.

It's important to know that both George Bush and Bill Clinton came from these groups. Bill Clinton and George Bush both belonged to the Bilderburgers, the Club of Rome, the Tri-Lateral Commission, and the Council on Foreign Relations. And I believe that these people dominate both of the major political parties, the Republicans and the Democrats. In fact, I call them Socialist Party A and Socialist Party B. The biggest push for the New World Order didn't come from the Democrats, it came from the Republicans through George Bush.

It is very likely that there are powerful people behind the scenes who are orchestrating world events to their advantage. The Clinton agenda could be the homosexualization of America, expansion of environmental controls, securing abortion rights, and expanded government regulations for more direct control over our lives.

If you want more insight into the direction our government is taking us read *Earth in the Balance: Ecology and the Human Spirit,* by then-Senator Al Gore.[1] It is not just about environmentalism, it is about the New Age plan for socializing America and the world. It is an incredible New Age document as well as an environmental document. Expansion of environmental controls are to be used as a vehicle for the socialization of America. It talks about the expansion of the size, power, and influence of the United Nations and its U.N. world army and the disarming of the American people via gun control.

We're moving rapidly towards total gun control in America. The propaganda blitz has been in effect for sometime to soften us up for more and more stringent gun control. In fact, if you look at the gun control laws of 1968 and the recent laws passed by Congress, you will find incredible parallels and similarities between those gun control laws and the gun control laws in Nazi Germany that were passed in 1928 and again in 1938.

New World Order

What is the New World Order? Is it something to be feared? George Bush has been on record of mentioning it by name several hundred times when he was president. *Business Week* ran an article titled, "On the Threshold of a New World Order" (Sept. 27, 1993, page 60). *Time* magazine carried an article about "Building a New World" (March 14, 1994, page 73-77).

The call for a New World Order goes way back. Fidel Castro talked about the New World Order in 1979 in his speech to the United Nations. Mikehail Gorbachev also spoke about wanting to build a New World Order.

The New World Order is simply a new world government. A world government under the control of something like the United Nations. The target date of implementation usually batted around is the year 2000. We do know from the Bible that this end-time world government will be replete with a one world currency, a one world central bank, and a one world religion.

The New World Order proponents believe that we should have one world economic planning, one world family planning and population control, and a one world environmental control — all held together by a one world army. In the March 6, 1992, issue of the *New York Times* an article discusses the New World army. This army is to be made up of troops from many different countries, including the United States. Have you noticed recently that for the first time in American history our troops are serving under United Nations commanders?

Another piece to the New World Order puzzle is to merge together the common interests of the United States and other world powers. You say, "Well, if we have common interests, is that all bad?" It's bad if we give up the freedom to govern ourselves here in the United States. NAFTA, Goals 2000, and GATT are but a few of the major moves that will eventually take the elective voice from the American people. In other words, our government is signing documents that agree to do what the world wants us to do, despite what we vote to do. For example, most of the world does not allow Christians to witness about their faith. Believe it or not, this is where we are headed with the New World Order.

Remember John Anderson running for president as an Independent in 1980? He asked for you to vote for him because he supported a U.N. World Federation. He felt that world peace required world laws. Global problems require global governments. Anderson was working to transform the United Nations into an empowered democrat world federation. He believed the only answer was a global parliament to enact laws to protect the earth's environment, complete with peace-keeping forces and world laws to prevent wars.

Regional World Governments

This U.N. version of the New World Order has three major regional governments. The first regional government is in western Europe, through the European Economic Community. If you go to Europe today, you'll find posters around Europe that say "Europe: Many tongues, one voice." These posters have a picture of the Tower of Babel in the middle. These posters also have many references to Satan such as goatheads, horns, and five-point stars with two points up instead of one. This leads me to the conclusion that the United States of Western Europe is into the occult. This is most interesting since the eventual Antichrist will have his power base in countries that make up the old Roman Empire!

The second of the regional governments of the New World Order is NACOM, the North American Common Market. That's made up of the United States, Canada, and Mexico. Like the European Economic Community, they will begin as an economic union and then eventually become a political union. NAFTA, with the dropping of trade barriers, is just the beginning. Eventually it won't be necessary to have borders, political divisions, etc.

The U.N. plan also has America divided into regional governments. There was legislation passed during the Nixon administration in 1972 that set up the future dispensation of 10 regional governments in America. If you live in Colorado, you're in region 8; Texas, region 6, California, region 9, etc. But regional governments can't exist until they make a major overhaul of the U.S. Constitution. This could only happen if Americans are dumb enough to fall for a constitutional convention to "rectify some of the injustices our founding fathers didn't anticipate 200 years ago," or some other impassioned plea. Regardless of the reason, the real plan behind a Constitutional Convention is to scrap the U.S. Constitution and to put in a new Constitution. In all likelihood, it's already been written. It was probably written several years ago for the explicit purpose of merging the United States into a world government, or the New World Order.

The third major regional government in the New World Order is headquartered in Tokyo, Japan, which would control the Pacific Rim.

There are more junior regional governments such as Latin America, Africa, in the Middle East, and the Southeast Pacific, etc.

Environmentalism

It's hard to argue against the environment, pollution, and the sincere desire to save our planet from ourselves. Christians, of course, realize we can't save the earth because God will destroy it. However, being good stewards of the resources God has given us, Christians should look for ways to conserve, recycle, etc. However, the movement to use the environment as a reason to pass extreme laws to restrict the rights of Americans is straight from the pit of hell.

What the Socialists, Communists and the New World Order promoters couldn't get through under the banner of Marxism/Leninism, or the hammer and the sickle, they're now trying to get through under the green banner of environmentalism. I'm not an environmentalist, but I am for clean air. I hate the smog in Los Angeles and other cities. I think most of us with common sense are for clean water and air. But what the government is doing is going way beyond common sense. They are using the environmental issue as an unopposed springboard to regulate every aspect of our family, business and private property, all under the guise of cleaning up the environment.

But the real reason is to use the environmental issue to move America under a world government. Remember the Earth Summit? The Earth Summit took place down in Rio de Janeiro in 1992. It was the biggest environmental clam bake in the history of the world, with 160 heads of state there. George Bush attended. The United States delegation was headed by then Senator Al Gore. The entire conference was dominated by supporters of the New World Order, New Agers, and leading occultists. It was sponsored by the United Nations who is openly using environmentalism scare tactics to move the nations of the earth under one voice.

George Bush talked about a new age of promise. When he talked about a "thousand points of light," it was lifted directly from the writings of Alice Bailey. Alice Bailey was an obvious occultist who lived in this country four decades ago. "A thousand Points of Light" also comes from the first line of a New Age mantra, which calls for the Lord Matrea to come to planet Earth. Some have even suggested that when George Bush talked about "a thousand points of light" that it was a message to New Agers around the world. Hopefully it was just his speech writer.

Spiritual Decline

The real reason America is in decline on a monetary, economic, social, and political basis is because America is in a spiritual decline. We, as a nation, have abandoned our spiritual, God-centered heritage, and switched to a man-centered culture that excludes God, Jesus Christ, the Bible, heaven and hell, and most absolutes — the foundations on which this great nation was built. It appears that 50 years of prosperity has led to our nation taking its eyes off God and our dependence on Him.

Alexander Solzhenitsyn was asked on BBC Television some years ago, "Why did the Russian people lose their freedom?" He thought for a minute and said, "Because we forgot God." Our nation, as a whole, has forgotten where we came from.

Look at what's happened to our country in just one generation. Christians can no longer engage in religious expression in public or even in public school systems, because they're told it's unconstitutional. Acts which the Bible regards as perversion and blatant sin are glorified in the media, in the halls of

Congress, and in our presidential administrations, as well as protected by the courts — all under the guise of equality.

If you believe what the Bible says about homosexuality, and what God says about it being an abomination to Him, you are politically incorrect, and you are in danger of committing a hate crime. That could even be ratified into law. If you teach your children what the Bible says about homosexuality, then not only will that be a hate crime, but it also could be defined, according to proposed legislation, as criminal child abuse. This, unfortunately, is possible unless America changes it's direction. It makes me want to cry over the fact our children may not know what it is like to grow up in a free country.

Morality

We all know the story — in one generation, over 30 million abortions. Incredible. It's condoned by government, paid for and defended with tax dollars, and rationalized as simply the free-choice elimination of an unwanted fetus instead of what the Bible calls murder — the shedding of innocent blood. Widespread euthanasia is destined to follow. The homosexual minority is protected from any criticism or restrictions, and if we make any criticism, then we are considered the bad guys.

What's happened to our morality and our culture in this country? Health and Human Services (HHS), our government's largest department, spearheads an aggressive safe-sex program designed to saturate American children from kindergarten through high school with immoral sexual propaganda. Most parents barely take notice. Italian Communist Party founder Antonio Gramshee strategized that if the morality and culture of a society can be destroyed, then that society can be easily brought down in a revolution.

Who is the highest-paid woman in America? Madonna — $60 million a year. You cannot print what she stands for. Who is the most popular and best-paid man in America? Michael Jackson. These are the people many of our teenagers are idolizing in this country. How far culturally, morally, and spiritually have we fallen? What's worse, an incredible number of Christian families let their children listen to this type of garbage music. If you listen to it, you probably wouldn't understand the words, but literally all of it promotes satanism, suicide, necrophilia, sex, drugs, or rebellion.

I believe there are four basic reasons why this incredible free-fall from our moral base is taking place.

First, powerful liberals, secular humanists, and committed socialists have intentionally subverted our morals, culture, and Christian traditions, primarily through the media and public education, in order to compromise America into a world government.

Second, Americans have become fat, dumb, and lazy after 50 years of uninterrupted prosperity. Good times don't breed good, strong character like tough times do. What kind of backbone did the average American have during World War II? Or World War I? Or the Great Depression? These were tough times that pulled together our families, or churches, and our nation.

Third, the American family has been saturated with almost 40 years of a steady diet of television. The average family watches between 40 and 50 hours of television a week in this country — most of it garbage. If you still have a television, I dare you to watch an hour of MTV. Pick any hour of the week and you will practically throw up. All you will see is sex, perversion, rebellion, and satanism — 24 hours a day!

Television is being used to effectively manipulate the American psyche. It is controlled by a group of people who want to move us toward this New World Order. Think about it, there are only four major networks: ABC, CBS, NBC, and CNN. Three major news magazines: *Newsweek, Time*, and *U.S. News & World Report*. And only a handful of newspaper chains. These few media sources control roughly 97 percent of the information the average American gets. And they're all controlled by a very narrow group of people who are determined to push us into this New World Order.

I have a friend who was in close contact with Bella Dodd. Bella Dodd had been on the national committee of the Communist party back during the late forties and early fifties. Dodd was also head of the New York State Teachers' Union. She said to my friend, long after she left the Communist party, "We Communists consider television to be one of the most valuable tools in the conquest of America."

My friend said, "Oh, you mean all the propaganda? All the twisting of the news and the distortion?"

But Dodd said, "No, that's not it. We've got our people in there. We've got our people who toe the line, etc. We saw television as a medium whereby we could influence a whole generation of Americans who would sit passively with their minds in neutral." She said while that was happening, "we planned to quietly come in and take over their country."

There's an interesting book out called *Target America*, written by James Tyson. He has a very respected intelligence background. The book explains the Soviet penetration of the U.S. media. Tyson believes that there are approximately 2,000 KGB agents working within the media in the United States.[2] General George Keegan, former head of the U.S. Air Force intelligence, said to me personally that he felt that there were as many as 50,000 KGB agents in the United States today!

I don't know if anybody actually knows how many agents are in the U.S., or involved with the media, but I do know that if you watch a lot of television your mind will become like mashed potatoes and you will not be able to think very deeply. I have seen people who were great thinkers, deep thinkers, discerners, and they started watching a lot of television, and of course, it's addictive, and they simply lost their ability to discern and think. So turn off your televisions! I know a family who actually had a ceremony. They took their television into the backyard and the father took a .357 magnum and, after praying for forgiveness for watching it so much, he plugged it six times right in the screen. Then they dug a hole and they buried it. He feels his life has been dramatically changed for the better.

Fourth, we don't fear God as a nation. There were 50 churches burned recently in an 18-month period in Florida. Let's hope this isn't a trend. We are in grave danger of seeing the beginning of persecution of true believers in the United States. In fact, there are Christians who are already being persecuted. There was a church in Colorado that was closed down because the pastor took a stand against a pro-homosexual ordinance. I know Christians who have been imprisoned. This is not just the pro-lifers who are taking a stand against the killing of the unborn who are being jailed. The Crime Control Bill has pages and pages of fine print that could be used to justify putting anyone in prison, anyone who does not agree with the New World Order.

There's a book out titled *When Time Shall Be No More: Prophecy Beliefs in Modern American Culture,* written by Paul Boyer.[3] I don't recommend you read it but you will be interested in what it says. Boyer is a professor of history at the University of Wisconsin. The book analyzes the Christian evangelical movement in this country. Virtually every leader in the Christian movement in this country is examined in great detail. And the conclusions to this book are that the greatest danger and threat to America and its continuing survival are the fundamental, evangelical, born-again Christians! It blames Christians for the Cold War, the arms race, crime in the streets, child abuse, homophobia, poverty, and virtually every problem and disease in this country.

In essence, the book claims that fundamental Christians are a very, very dangerous group. A parallel is drawn between the growing Christian influence in politics to the fact people didn't notice how dangerous the Nazis were until they were in power. Christians are portrayed as a great lurking danger in America. Normally you could write this off as just a fringe book. But this book is being quoted all over the country in the media. When the liberal press talks about Christians, and wants to label them as dangerous religious cultists, they quote from this book. This type of book, quoted to 97 percent of America through the media, could lay the philosophical base for persecution of Christians in America.

Immediately after the attack against the Branch Davidians in Waco, Texas, the national media began to ask the question, "How can you recognize a dangerous religious cultist?" Their answer will shock you. A cultist was described as someone who studies the Bible with emphasis on Bible prophecy and the return of Jesus Christ, home schools children, disciplines children through spanking, has guns, and believes in survival food. Does that describe anybody you know?

Two days after Waco there was an article in *USA Today* (April 21, 1993) that read, "Experts Weighing How to Deal With Cults in the Future." It said, "Today these groups tend to believe that the Bible predicts the end of the world is near. 'In the past decade, we've had a sharp upsurge in interest in Bible prophecy,' said historian Paul Boyer, author of a study, 'When Time Shall Be No More.' Boyer said that such seemingly unrelated events as the Israelis gaining control of Jerusalem in 1967, the threat of nuclear war, and shifts in the global economy are seen as signs that the cultists see that, as prophesied in the Bible, the end is near and Jesus Christ will return." This means that if you believe Jesus Christ will return in the not-too-distant future, you have just been re-defined by *USA Today, The New York Times*, and others as a "dangerous religious cultist." If we allow this type of thinking to prevail, it's easy to see the potential for persecution of the Christian church in the United States.

Pray It Doesn't Happen

In case you haven't figured this out, there are a lot of people who don't like born-again evangelical fundamental Christians. The New Agers hate us be-cause they realize that we will not adapt once the Age of Aquarius dawns upon us. The pro-New World Order groups don't like Christians because we under-stand where the one world government leads. The environmentalists think that Christians aren't con-cerned for the earth and don't buy into their "over population" theories. The homosexuals sure don't like us because of what the Bible says about their lifestyle. The women's libbers don't like us. The pro-choice crowd can't stand us. The secular humanists despise us.

Our post-Christian culture, as Frances Schaeffer called it, is turning dramatically and rapidly against Christians and especially born-again, evan-gelical Christians. I believe that in the future it's very possible that we will be forced into making some difficult decisions. How bad it may actually become, I don't know. But it is not too far-fetched to analyze other countries in the world today to get a perspective of how bad it could become. Things like loss of tax-exempt status, having churches closed down for preaching things that are termed "anti-government," underground or home church situations, and laws passed specifically forbidding you from telling someone about your faith. Pray that this never happens in America — because it just might.

10

Dead Ahead — What to Watch, What to Do

Chuck Missler

One of the things that should really grab our attention is the bizarre movements in the United States and the predicament this country is in.

This predicament really accrues from three primary drives. Speaking financially first, it accrues from the government debt. Everybody needs to do their homework on the federal debt. Notice I didn't say deficit. I'm amazed at how many prominent people in the media confuse the deficit and the debt. If you reduce the deficit to zero, we still don't make it because of the compounding interest on our federal debt. We do not have the cash flow to pay the interest.

The debt, the existing debt — don't let anyone discuss this subject with you who doesn't talk about it quantitatively; don't be misled by the arm-waving. Take the trouble to get a perspective, a broad perspective of the numbers, and they will startle you.

Of course, on top of that, we make it worse each year with the deficit. The federal picture is only one of three aspects financially. The corporate predicament of firms in this country is in dire straits; they are overloaded with debt because of the excesses of the eighties. We invented a new parlor game in the eighties called leveraged buy-outs. It's interesting — if you read any economic text, you'll discover that, typically, businesses borrow money to accomplish an objective: they develop new products, open new lines of distribution, or expand production facilities. Also, in the eighties we invented a way for a healthy company to borrow money and have no benefit by it. They just used the money to buy out the shareholders. It's an interesting ploy for the guys who could pull it off. But on the other hand, you take a healthy, strong, vital corporation, and when the smoke clears, you have exactly the same corporation with the same products, same distribution channel, same facilities, loaded to the ears with debt. This same company will now struggle over the coming years simply to pay off that debt and let the new owners own it without having put up anything significant at risk.

It was an interesting game to play in the eighties, but the net result on our industrial establishment has been disastrous. Those companies that weren't taken over were loaded with debt to prevent being taken over. The net result, as we now discover, much to our amazement, is that they're now non-competitive on the international marketplace because their competitors abroad have new plans and modern research. Of course, research and new product development are the first things to go in the pursuit of paying off debt. So the dilemma we have is not just at the federal level.

That's probably the most severe and also the most intractable to remedy, but our corporate scene is no worse; our industrial base, which supports everything, is in serious shape. That's why the smart entrepreneurs are doing their entrepreneuring off-shore, not in the U.S. Because if you're in electronics, it's insane to create an electronics company in the United States. Your suppliers, your customers, and your source of capital are all in Asia; no reason to be here. And on it goes. So the corporate environment is a serious one. Keep an eye on the business page of your daily papers and keep an eye on the companies that are laying off employees even though they have previously been proud of never having a lay-off. Keep an eye on corporate printings and discover what's really happening.

Of course, the third level is ourselves, our own personal debt. There are steps we can take to deal with this on an individual level, but, as a nation, our personal debt is part of the overall problem.

So we're heading into an environment that is characterized by upheaval and uncertainty. Let's just try to strip away the detail and focus on the fundamentals. No competent analyst can deny that a major upheaval in the United States is inevitable. Not likely; certain. And that accrues, of course, from the fact that even the most superficial analysis of our predicament demonstrates that a change is coming.

The problem is that while an upheaval is certain, there are two things that we do not know. First, we don't know what form it will take. There are really good, competent experts who believe we're heading to a very, very severe depression or deflation. There are other very competent analysts who believe we're going to plunge into hyper-inflation.

Those two disasters are both disasters, but opposites in many ways. Many people clearly map out the parallels between ourselves and Argentina and Germany and other recent, historical examples. And you can make a good case for either one of these. The problem is they're opposites. But the main point is that there is major upheaval forthcoming.

All of the institutions in this country that we've come to rely on as part of our stability should be regarded as suspect, but go carefully. Let me give an example of what I mean. If you go to Europe, or any sophisticated foreign environment, the people who bank there will always watch closely the financial statements of the institution with whom they're dealing. In the United States, we are notorious for ignoring them. How many of us have examined the balance sheet of the bank we're dealing with? The reason people don't: "Well, my account's insured by the FDIC, the Federal Deposit Insurance Corporation." They're broke. No big secret. Does that mean we're totally at risk? Well, not in the near-term sense, perhaps, because Congress is going to have to patch, but the net of it is that the FDIC is no real serious comfort.

That's why most sophisticated investors don't put major liquid assets in banks anyway, they use other forms. And that's why most sophisticated investors I know bank off-shore with one of the major, powerful banks in any of the major capitals. They all have advantages and disadvantages and there are specialists who deal in picking those.

As we face this issue we're confronted with two problems. We don't know the form of coming upheaval. There's a second thing we don't know. We don't know the timing. There are those, including some senators and other perceptive analysts, who believe the upheaval could be very close. All kinds of indicators highlight that we're way over-extended and a major disruption is overdue.

So there are the doomsday types who believe the economy can collapse within months. On the other side of the coin, it's also clear that we should never underestimate the ability of the Congress and the Senate to forestall at great expense the coming debacle, inventing all kinds of ways to confiscate assets to forestall the coming crash. So it could be several years.

The point is, we don't know the timing; we don't know the form it will take. If you're a military strategist, any time you face uncertainty, your strategy is always mobility. In the financial sense, that equates to liquidity.

It's interesting that all the competent advisors I know, including Don McAlvany and Larry Burkett, suggest: Step 1: Get out of debt. Now by this, I am not talking about collateralized loans on productive assets. That's a form of financial structure that's a separate subject. And, incidentally, a modest home with a mortgage is a collateralized loan on a productive asset. I'm really talking about those states in which they do not have deficiency judgment. In other words, the worst you can do is lose your home. Some states have deficiency judgments, which means you're liable for the entire balance even after they take your home.

The point is, what I'm talking about is personal debt. Get out of debt.

How do you do that? There's a formula. Just 4 points: Point 1: lower your cost of living. It's your primary discretionary freedom. Many things are going to happen to you; there are few things you can really alter. The one thing you can control, painful though it may be, is to lower your cost of living. Don't depend on a rising income to somehow pad or repair. Lower your cost of living. Simplify. Make a budget, not of dollars, of time. Sit down with a pad and paper and figure out over some incremental period of time where you spend your time. What's really dear to you? What do you really enjoy? And see if your capital investments match that.

Many of us have indulgences that we really don't have the time to enjoy. Get rid of them. Simplify. If you have indulgences that you spend a lot of time on and they're important to you, no problem. Acknowledge it and put it in front of you. But do a budget of your time and then attack your financial structure and where you're spending and try to find a way to get back to the essentials. Figure out where you get the most bang for your buck, so to speak, in terms of your personal lifestyle and fulfillment.

Point 2: The urgent thing to do is create a positive delta between what you've got coming in and what's going out, and then use that delta first of all to get out of debt. Why? Because the Bible says the borrower's the slave to the lender.

Debt is contrary to God's plan for your life. One of the many ways that He leads you is through the resources that He makes available, and when you borrow, you end-run His leading. So if you're really serious about seeking the will of God, you don't end-run His resources by borrowing. I'm speaking at the personal level, I'm not talking about financial structures on productive assets.

So lower your costs of living, get out of debt. That leads to point 3. I personally believe that the third step in your strategy is to "guard your liquidity." What do I mean by that? Well, in order to guard your liquidity, you need to know who its enemies are. Well, who's enemy number one? The government.

Congress is faced with a deadly trap. It has to find the cash-flow to pay the interest on existing debts. And it can't do it from tax revenue. The current debt requires over 60 percent of the total personal income tax and it's growing because the debt is compounding faster than our productivity by a significant factor. So the Congress, the Ways and Means people, have to find a way to shore up this mess. And the only way they can do it is by confiscating assets. There's a limit to what they can do in taxation. Even with the onerous taxes that are being thrown at us, there won't be enough to solve that problem. So they've got to find ways of confiscation.

One of the ways is called the EPA, because they now have financial incentives to create EPA levies on corporations that can't pay, so they go through a Chapter 11 reorganization where the government owns a major chunk of those assets. They call it the Superfund. Another one of those cases uses the environmental banner to mask brutal, incentived confiscation of assets. Corporations know about this because there are big dollars involved there. As you watch the trauma of these major corporations trying to zig and zag under some of those levies, recognize what's really going on. It's a confiscation problem in which all the principals on the side of the government are in effect on incentives. But it's also, as it gets more and more desperate, going to be reaching deeper and deeper, and the only assets around will end up being yours and mine. So that's a problem.

But there's another dimension in this country. I have had the privilege of spending most of my corporate life doing international ventures. In fact, I was on a board in Colorado Springs that was part of a public company in Australia. When the Australians first came into America, they could not believe the way American businessmen have to operate in the litigative environment in this country. In the United States, there are 50 attorneys for every engineer. In

Japan, there are 50 engineers for every attorney. There are more attorneys in Washington, DC, than there are in all of Japan.

The problem in this country is that we have a litigative environment already, and I believe it's going to get much worse because anybody in this country can sue anybody else. Every lawsuit is a roulette wheel. Talk to your legally trained friends and if they're competent litigators, they'll tell you the following, in effect. No matter what the fact situation is, you can't predict the outcome of a lawsuit. A competent litigator will tell you that you have a better or less than 50-50 chance of winning. It's a roulette wheel. So anybody can sue anybody. A lawsuit has a life of its own and can lead to, what's called in the trade, the unworthy judgment.

Suppose somebody looks on the tax rolls and sees that you have your home free and clear and that it's worth a lot of money. And suppose he's hungry — this is a lawyer with time on his hands because things have gotten rougher. So he contrives a claim against you, slips on your doorstep, whatever, and you find yourself in a lawsuit. You get hit with what's called an unworthy judgment. Unfair. But there is a guy with a gun and a badge on your doorstep with a judgment of $10 million against you. What do you do about that? By the time that happens, very little can be done,

It happens every day and it will happen with increasing frequency. But I'm going to suggest to you that you give some thought to protecting your liquidity. You do that several ways. If you have consequential assets, I strongly encourage consultation with a specialist in this area, an attorney who specializes not just in estate planning in terms of typical estate concerns, but in what's called creditor strategy. If you have a consequential estate, you may want to first of all break it into pieces. You may want to explore trusts and other forms of protection, but the ultimate strategy here is to own nothing. You don't have to be stripped of indulgences to do that, but what you do not own generally can't be taken away from you. And when the guy's on your doorstep with a gun and a badge with that $10 million judgment, you say, "Well, here, take my Seiko. That's all I own, goodbye." Now that's not trivial to set up, but it need not be prohibitively expensive if you're talking about consequential assets. So you'll want to consult with specialists who know how to structure your estate in ways that give you at least some protection against the chicanery artists.

The other way you guard your liquidity is to apply what the Bible suggests. If you follow the writings of Solomon, you know that you want to diversify. And when you build a little chart for yourself, a little matrix, what you're talking about is having some of your assets invested in currencies, but not necessarily U.S. alone. You're also talking about having some of your assets in very short-term maturities. Liquidity isn't necessarily cash or cash equivalents, it's short-term maturities. Nothing long-term, and certainly not equities unless you're a professional speculator.

One way to have this handled for you is through professional management. There are 3,000 mutual funds available and you can't do this simply. You've got to spend a little time and find out what kinds there are, and you'll discover there's every conceivable kind of fund around. Some specialize just in currencies, some specialize in short-term notes, and there are any number of constraints that can be applied to one or the other of them. Many of them managed in the United States invest entirely abroad; many are managed abroad; many invest only in government bonds. Mention any category and you'll find a mutual fund that will achieve that objective in a plurality of alternatives by professionals. The assets are held by a third party, so they're generally fairly immune to gains among themselves — but they do require some study. However, they're highly desirable as a vehicle; often overlooked because they can be quite flexible. With a telephone call, you can actually shift your assets from A to B to C, so they're very flexible. Mutual funds can also be, if properly chosen, very inexpensive in terms of overhead costs, so you might want to explore this. But one of the things you want to do, I believe, is diversify whatever it is you do have in such a way as to protect yourself against the vicissitudes of an uncertain horizon.

I have mentioned that the Vortex Strategy, as we'll call it, has four points: 1) lower your cost of living; 2) get out of debt; 3) guard your liquidity. But there's a fourth step. I leave it to the fourth because it's the most important: Learn the supernatural aspects of stewardship.

Find out from the Bible what God's purposes are for money. Make a list of all the little rubrics and ideas, the top 10 worldly principles of managing your money. You'll be shocked to discover, if you make a column of God's purposes, they're almost opposite. What are our purposes? To be financially independent. What's God's purpose? To have you dependent on Him. And so on. Our purposes are self-oriented; our concept is to have personal freedom. God's agenda is to have you personally responsible.

I know you've heard this before, but there is a very strange challenge in the Bible. All through the Bible one of the so-called unpardonable sins, just as a rhetorical phrase, is that you never tempt God. You'll find that all through the Old Testament and New Testament. In fact, Jesus Christ in the famed incident of the three temptations, said, "Thou shalt not tempt the Lord thy God" (Matt. 4:7;KJV).

But there's an interesting exception where God dares you to dare Him. In Malachi 3:10, He challenges you with respect to the tithes. He says, "Prove me now herewith . . . if I will not open you the windows of heaven and pour you out a blessing that there shall not be room enough to receive it" (KJV). It's strange that the God of the universe would put himself in that kind of a box, that the God of the universe would challenge you to call His bluff. The tithe is not an offering. The tenth is His. You don't give an offering until you've already fulfilled that commitment. I know of no person who's tried it who hasn't been blown away by what God did in their life.

Wherever you are financially, there is a God in control watching every moment. He loves you so much He can't take His eyes off you and He's there most visibly when you need Him the most. In fact, a friend of mine on Wall Street once told me, in a slightly different context, "Chuck, if your biggest problems are money problems, you're in great shape." God is a God of healing no matter what the situation is.

It's interesting to watch as the U.S. braces for what's ahead. Many predict anarchy as joblessness increases, as the state revenues decline because of the lack of income, and the services get squeezed so there aren't funds for police protection at the local level. The L.A. riots were just the beginning. Watch across the country. I watch California, not just because we've just recently moved from there, but because I think California is a leading indicator of the national predicament. California, in addition to all the federal burden, has its own excesses of welfare state issues and other problems. It is also suffering brutally because of the exodus of its revenue base, both in people and in businesses. So watch California to get a fore-taste of what's coming.

As the local revenues decline and the services erode, joblessness increases and individuals' financial predicaments become more severe. As people cast about for someone to blame, you can expect racism and scapegoating.

So as we look at all of these signs around us, it's logical to wonder where we are on God's time-table. And if you're really interested in knowing what time it is on God's clock, there is a sure-fire way to find out. You always look at Israel.

In this context, there is something that I think

is very dramatic in front of us. Three times in the New Testament it mentions that the temple will be rebuilt. Jesus mentioned it, Paul mentioned it, and John mentioned it. So people who take the Bible seriously have been looking for the rebuilding of the temple in Jerusalem. And the exciting thing is that they are preparing to rebuild.

The primary obstacle to the rebuilding is an uncertainty over the exact location of Solomon's Temple and Herod's Temple, as well as the current presence of the Muslim Dome of the Rock.

As far as location is concerned, there are three basic theories today, the Dome of the Rock being the traditional one held by many top rabbis. The position to the north is held by many Christians, but there's a third theory that's also gaining some interest. That is the possibility that the temple stood to the south of the Dome of the Rock. In resolving these questions, many intent observers are keeping an eye on the research being done with ground-penetrating radar and the thermographic, or infrared, fly-bys.

The point is, Israel is back in her land and very real preparations are being made for the rebuilding of the temple.

That tells us a lot about where we are on God's prophetic timetable, and it once again confirms that we are living in the most exciting period in all of history.

That leads me to a challenge. The real issue in all of this is that you have a personal relationship with the Lord Jesus Christ. I encourage you, if you haven't made a decision for Jesus Christ, avail yourself of the eligibility that He has purchased for you for all eternity. Then make that profession and share that commitment with someone you trust spiritually.

I also have one other challenge. I'd like for you to think for a moment about your favorite hobby. Let me tell you a few things that I suspect about your hobby. First of all, you probably spend more on it than you want your spouse to find out. And you probably know more about your hobby than you know about your profession. You stay on top of it. It's fun; it's a labor of love.

So I have rather a peculiar challenge that I'd like you to consider. I'd like you to consider making the Bible your hobby. I believe that you have no chance of understanding CNN or whatever news services you have unless you know your Bible. I do not believe you'll understand the coming events of the next few weeks, the next few months, the next few years, unless you have a competent biblical perspective.

God will supernaturally communicate to you through this book. Indeed, in many counselors there is wisdom, but the Lord's primary way of communicating is through His Word, and He will leap out at you through your readings and your study. And the more you study, the more the pieces will fit together.

I have a Bible verse that's become one of my favorites, Habakkuk 1:5. "Behold among the nations, and regard, and wonder marvelously, for I will work a work in your days, which ye will not believe, though it be told you."

So in conclusion, after looking at much of the

broad political spectrum, I'd like to confess that I am neither a Democrat nor a Republican, but a monarchist. And I would like to share with you just a few things about the King I serve.

My King is King of the Jews. He's a racial King. My King is the King of Israel. He's a national King. My King is the King of all ages. He's the King of heaven, the King of glory, the King of kings and the Lord of lords. Do you know Him?

The heavens declare His glory, the firmament showeth His handiwork. He who is and who was and who always will be, He's the first and the last, the alpha and the omega, the A and the Z. He is the first fruits of them that slept. He is the I Am that I Am. He's the voice of the burning bush. He's the captain of the Lord's hosts, He's the conqueror of Jericho. By Him were all things made that were made. Without Him, was not anything made that was made. And by Him all things are held together. In Him dwells the fullness of the Godhead bodily. The very God of gods. He is our kinsman redeemer.

He's also our avenger of blood. He's our city of refuge. He's our performing high priest, our personal Prophet, and our reigning King. He's enduringly strong, He's entirely sincere, He's eternally merciful. He's immortally graceful, He's imperially powerful. He stands alone in himself. He's august, He's preeminent, He's supreme, He's unique, He's unparalleled. He's the loftiest idea in literature. He's the highest personality in philosophy. He's the fundamental doctrine of theology. He's the supreme problem in higher criticism. He's God's Son.

There is no means of measuring His limitless love. He's the only One able to supply all our needs simultaneously. No barriers can hinder him from pouring out His blessings. He's available to the tempted and the tried. He blesses the young. He cleanses the lepers. He defends the feeble. He delivers the captives. He delivers the debtors. He forgives the sinners. He franchises the meek. He guards the besieged. He heals the sick. He provides strength to the weak. He regards the aged. He rewards the diligent. He serves the unfortunate. He sympathizes and He saves.

He's the captain of the conquerors, the centerpiece of civilization, the doorway of deliverance, the governor of governors, the head of the heroes, the highway of holiness, the king of knowledge, the master of the mighty, the overseer of overcomers, the pathway of peace, the roadway of righteousness, the sinner's Saviour, the well-spring of wisdom, the prince of princes, King of kings, and Lord of lords.

His goodness is limitless. His grace is sufficient. His light is matchless. His love is never-changing. His mercy is everlasting. His offices are manifold. His promises are sure. His reign is righteous. His Word is enough. His yoke is easy, and His burden is light. I wish I could describe Him to you. He's indescribable. He's incomprehensible. He's irresistible, He's invincible. The heaven of heavens cannot contain Him; man cannot explain Him. You can't get Him out of your mind, you can't get Him off of your hands. You can't outlive Him and you can't live without Him.

The Pharisees couldn't stand Him and learned

they couldn't stop Him. Herod couldn't kill Him. Death couldn't handle Him, the grave couldn't hold Him. He has always been and always will be. He had no predecessor and will have no successor. You can't impeach Him, and He isn't going to resign. His is the Kingdom and the power and the glory forever and ever. Amen.

11

Fourteen Ways to "Steel" against the Future

Don McAlvany

We're witnessing the death of not only human rights in America, but also property rights. Any government agent or agency in America today can seize almost any property, and there's very little the citizen can do to protect himself. Property rights are very important and were guaranteed to us in our Constitution. In 1984 government seizures of so-called "illegal assets" totaled $30 million, in 1991 they were $644 million, and in 1992 they exceeded $800 million. Since 1985 the government asset forfeiture office boasted over $2.5 billion dollars in U.S. citizens' assets that have been seized. Over 80 percent of these seizures never resulted in an arrest or conviction. This indicates that most of the people and assets are being taken from innocent people. According to *USA Today,* there are now 1,000 forfeitures per week in the United States, or 52,000 per year.

What Assets?

What is the government seizing from American citizens? Assets seized, in order of frequency, are cash and other monetary instruments, vehicles, boats, planes, bank and brokerage accounts, real estate, and pension and profit-sharing plans. Asset forfeiture is clearly an unconstitutional process, though considered to be legal by the government. The process is unconstitutional when it allows any agency of the government to simply suspect you of a crime, not formally charge you, and then seize your property. In a chilling comparison, in Nazi Germany they seized people's property, jailed, and finally killed them . . . and it was all legal. Because something is legal does not mean that it is right, just, constitutional, or biblical.

What is happening is that the government is passing thousands of laws, rules, and regulations and then enforcing the law. But what if these new laws and regulations are unconstitutional? Or unbiblical? That's the problem we're faced with today. In most instances of property confiscation, there is no arrest, trial, or conviction. You are presumed guilty until you can prove yourself innocent, and that's not the way the Constitution was written. A great majority of the people who have had their property seized by the police are innocent and law-abiding. One study showed that in 80 percent of the seizures, the police never even filed charges against the victims of the seizures, or in some cases, filed charges and then dropped them.

The police need no warrant to seize your property. With no due process, they don't even have to formally charge you with the crime. There are hundreds of local, state, and federal laws and thousands of regulations on the books under which the government can now seize your property. Under these forfeiture/seizure laws, the government or police can seize your property with 100, or even 1,000 times the value of the maximum fine for the alleged offense, and they don't even have to convict you to do it. These seizures are legalized thefts by those who are supposed to be upholding the law, and give you a hint at the mindset of government agents, bureaucrats, and the police today. The government and police do not have to show any more than probable cause that a crime has been committed, the same standard which for centuries has been applied to search warrants. The police can now seize your home with no more evidence than it once took to search your home.

"Probable cause" is a legal term and it can be applied when the government suspects, not "knows" or "proves," racketeering. This could mean almost anything: drug possession, drug trafficking, money-laundering, robbery, murder, tax evasion, extortion, environmental crimes, violation of the Trading with the Enemy Act, violation of the Emergency Economic Powers Act, or gun control violations.

Finder's fees of 10 to 25 percent of the value of

the assets seized are regularly paid out to informants. *USA Today* has said that in 1992, 65 informants made over $100,000 each by simply alleging to police agencies that friends, neighbors, and/or business associates had committed crimes. When you go to trial, you do not have the right to confront the informant in court. The reason is that it's a civil, not a criminal, proceeding. According to the *Pittsburgh Press,* over 80 percent of the victims of 25,000 seizures which they analyzed were never accused of any crime. How can they seize people's assets and not even accuse them of a crime? This is simply unconstitutional.

Don't Look Suspicious

Looking suspicious when making a deposit at your local bank is one way you can get your assets seized. There's a box at the top of the cash transaction report, called the CTR. If a person looks nervous, protests having the form filled out, or is too inquisitive about the form, then that box is checked. The bank then notifies the Treasury Department. By law, they cannot tell you. Should the Treasury Department determine your actions *suspicious*, it can freeze your assets. It's then up to you to prove that the seizure is improper. How do you hire an attorney if they've frozen all of your financial assets? This happens every day.

Forfeiture laws were expanded in 1984 to allow the government to seize assets without first charging the owner. The proceeds from these seizures finance more investigations and are helping to finance the financial shortfall of local, state, and federal governments. Elimination of the need to prove a crime has moved most action to civil courts, where the government accuses the item, not the owner, of being tainted by crime. As a result, jury trials can be refused, illegal searches condoned, and rules of evidence ignored. Again — in 80 percent of the seizure cases, no charges are filed. If they are filed, you have plenty of time to fight them. But when no charges are filed, the action is a civil seizure/forfeiture, you only have a limited time to fight the seizure. In California, you would have only 10 days.

For example, suppose you are accused of having grown marijuana plants in your backyard. But they check and find that the plants are not there. But they testify you were doing some gardening last week and the government says they were there. They can seize your house, even from a tip from an unnamed informant, based on the fact you had marijuana in your backyard. Probable cause was simply the tip.

When they seize your home you have 10 days to prove that you didn't do anything wrong. Now, how do you prove that you didn't do anything wrong? How do you prove that you didn't do something you didn't do? In the forfeiture hearings, there is no presumption of innocence — you are presumed guilty until you prove you're innocent. In a criminal trial, you simply have to raise reasonable doubt as to your guilt, but in a police forfeiture hearing, you have a positive burden to prove your innocence.

Who profits from the assets seized? If an informant was involved, he is paid 10 to 25 percent of the proceeds tax free. Tax free — isn't that interesting? The remaining balance is typically split 70 percent to the local police, the district attorney's office, and the judge's chamber with the Feds splitting the rest. If it was a federal seizure, the Feds will keep up to 70 percent of the proceeds. So whoever seizes the asset gets to keep the major portion. The traditional American concept of the police and courts, that justice is meant to be impartial, would all recoil at the idea that the police, the prosecuting and district attorneys, or judges have a direct financial stake in the outcome of a case. Yet under these seizure laws, that is exactly what happens.

This is how Third World officials have been corrupted over the years, and how they have stolen to enrich themselves. But not in America! We are entering an unconstitutional, socialist quagmire of seizures, forfeitures, and lawsuits of incredible proportions. The government encourages Americans to spy on one another for pay. The government and police unconstitutionally seize and confiscate private property of innocent American citizens as if we have no property rights. Americans who believe in constitutional guarantees to privacy or simply use cash are treated like criminals.

Of course, not all of the government officials or agents are on the take. Most believe in the Constitution. So this does not describe everybody in the police or government agencies, but it does describe a growing number of people who are mis-using this incredible new power to seize assets, and who in fact are finding it easier to go against honest, law-abiding citizens than to go against real criminals. I'm for crime control, but I believe I know what a criminal is.

A criminal is somebody who robs a bank, is an extortionist, a rapist, a murderer, a drug dealer, etc. A criminal is not an honest, law-abiding citizen who has stumbled over some unknown government regula-tion, had his assets seized, and is then thrown in jail.

Watch the Laws

Criminal terrorism is now a new category of crime. Most of us would consider criminal terrorism as an act of blowing up the Federal Building in Oklahoma City, the World Trade Center, or Pan-Am Flight 103. But that's not what the new Crime Control Act says. It's not about controlling crime, it's about putting restrictions on free speech, free assembly, and the freedom to publish and write things that are critical to the government. It's about stopping or coercing government policy and intimidation of the populace. It's about coming against demonstrators.

Under the new Crime Control Bill, Martin Luther King would have been declared to be a crimi-nal terrorist and would have drawn a very long prison sentence. Non-violent pro-life demonstrators can now be classified as criminal terrorists. So can homo-sexual demonstrators in Washington. So can those participating in an organized labor strike. Radio broad-casts which are critical of the government or govern-ment policy, by Jim Dobson, Hal Lindsey, or Don McAlvany can be labeled terrorism. Watch how they use these laws in the future.

The RICO racketeering statutes were passed some years ago to arrest organized crime figures. In recent years we've seen them applied against pro-life demonstrators. Now they're beginning to expand the definition under the Crime Control Bill to include almost any kind of political activity. More than one offense in any four-year period will qualify as terrorism. A pro-life demonstration can be ruled a terrorist activity. Now they will tell you, "Oh, well, we would never use it that way." Watch what the politicians do, not what they say.

Part of the Crime Control Act is penalties for the violation of the Emergency Economic Powers Act, up to one million dollars. Freedom of what you can say about what's going on in the economy is now curtailed. Security personnel at airports must notify law enforcement agencies if a traveler has over $10,000 in cash. After all, we know that's a dangerous crime.

The government has expanded civil criminal penalties, and penalties for civil rights violations like discrimination. For example if you refuse to hire a homosexual in your business, church, or Christian organization your actions will be considered a criminal activity or even terrorism. As strange as it sounds, that could easily happen with the new legislative interpretations coming.

Through public education it's easy to change children's' values and heavily influence them toward worldly ideals. That's why education was left up to the states in our Constitution. They realized if you could get them when they're young, you could turn them against family, erase the old history, give them new history, and then control the next generation.

John Dewey came along. He's considered to be the father of public education in America. He said, on a Colorado radio program, "Look, we want to destroy the influence of the Church and the family on children. We'll get them in the public school system, we'll get them out of the house at 7 or 7:30 in the morning, we'll keep them in school all day, we'll give them our information. They'll go to bed at 10 o'clock, their family will have seen them 30 minutes a day, and in a generation or two we will have broken the family's and the Church's hold on the children." People like this believe the government owns your children and has the right to tell you how to raise them, or take them from you and raise them themselves.

Traditional parents are now being redefined as child abusers. The Book of Proverbs says that if you love your children, you will give them proper discipline with the rod. But that's not politically correct today. You can actually be jailed for disciplining your children. The United Nations Convention on the Rights of the Child already says that to spank a child is criminal child abuse.

The American Economic Decline

The reason we're in an economic decline, which is going to accelerate into a depression at some point in the future, is because in the last 10 to 15 years we've been on the biggest debt binge in the history of the world. From George Washington through Jimmy Carter, we went from $0 to $3 trillion in debt. We made it by 1980. From 1980 to 1993, we went from $3 trillion in debt to $16 trillion, a five-and-one-half-fold increase in about 13 years, and despite the promises, it's still climbing. Consumer debt has tripled from

1980 to $3.5 trillion. Over the past 10 years, credit card debt has gone from $50 billion to $185 billion. Eighty percent of real estate is mortgaged. The average U.S. household debt is now 84 percent of annual income. That's a historical high.

In 1929, debt service was 10 percent of income; today it is 25 percent of income. Corporate debt tripled over the past decade from $700 billion to $2.5 trillion, and climbing. In 1930, corporations had 70 cents cash for every dollar in short-term debt that was due within 12 months. Today, corporations have only nine cents cash to cover each dollar in short-term debt, an 87 percent drop in short-term debt coverage since 1929 at the kick-off of the Great Depression.

U.S. government debt is out of control. If you add up all U.S. government debt, off-budget federal debts, state and local, real estate mortgages, corporate, consumer, and government guarantees to the banks and S & Ls, we're looking at a $21 trillion debt pyramid in the United States. When that debt pyramid falls, and cracks are spreading each day, it will easily send us into a depression — only much bigger than the Great Depression of the 1930s.

There will be severe consequences of the great American debt binge. Our foreign debt is $700 billion. We are now the largest debtor nation in the world and the borrower always becomes the servant to the lender. We will become servant to the world and will have to do what they want us to do. We will not be able to vote out the lenders because we don't like them.

There have been more corporate and private bankruptcies in recent years than at any time since the peak of the Great Depression. Personal bankruptcies have been growing, and reached over one million of your fellow Americans. Many, unfortunately, were Christians. There were over 100,000 businesses and corporations which went bankrupt, a record since the peak of the Great Depression. We've seen 2,000 banks and about 2,000 savings and loans fail in recent years, all as a result of too much debt.

There are consequences to our actions. If you jump off a tall building, you're going to eventually hit bottom. You may hope you don't, but the course chosen was irreversible. America is not much different. The course chosen is unlikely to change and the inevitable *will* happen. It's just a matter of time. All the manipulations of the federal government and the federal reserves trying to hold it together will, at some point in the future, fail. To me it already looks like we are in a slow-motion crash right now.

Alternate Sources

It's imperative that you understand that every government administration lies about virtually all economic statistics. They may say that unemployment is under 7 percent when it is actually closer to 11 percent; 50 percent higher. They may tell you that inflation is around 3 or 4 percent, when true Inflation is somewhere in the 9 to 11 percent range. Don't ever rely on what they are telling you because it's probably not true, or at best, severely filtered truth. You need to find some alternate sources of information. There are several good economic and political newsletters written from a conservative and a biblical perspective.

In 1980 the federal deficit (not to be confused with the Federal debt) was $72.2 billion and all personal income taxes collected by the government were $244 billion. The deficit was 29.8 percent of the total personal income taxes. In 1992 the estimated deficit was $449 billion and personal taxes collected, $478.7 billion. The deficit is now 93.8 percent of the personal income taxes collected. The government is now spending almost twice as much as it takes in, in taxes. The interest on the national debt costs $300 billion per year. That's 62 percent of all personal taxes collected. Within 5 to 8 percent, the interest on the national debt will rise to $600 billion, and more than all personal and corporate income taxes collected. Naturally this can't go on forever.

The only way to stop the impending depression is to dramatically lower taxes *and* cut government spending. Look at how our deficit has risen: Under Johnson, an average of $8.9 billion per year; under Nixon, $11 billion per year; under Ford, $63 billion a year; under Carter, $56 billion a year; under Reagan, $167 billion a year; under Bush, $260 billion a year; and under Clinton it will average even higher!

The optimists believe that there is inflationless prosperity as far ahead as we can see. This is what Wall Street and Washington says, and that's the majority view in this country. The deflationists say, "No, no. Look at the cracks that are spreading throughout the system. Look at the incredible record numbers of personal and corporate bankruptcies, bank and S & L failures, insurance company failures; we're going over the edge. We're going over Niagara Falls without our barrel." And they may have a point.

Now We're Relaxed

In the Old Testament, the Jews celebrated the year of Jubilee once every 50 years. They were commanded to liquidate all debt and start over from scratch. The problem is that every two to three generations, we forget and repeat our mistakes. God used a simple remedy.

Think about our own country. We were very conservative after the depression. Then we relaxed and began borrowing for our homes on 30-year mortgages instead of 7-year mortgages. Then we began borrowing for cars. Then appliances. Then just money for general expenses. Consolidation loans. Even the equity in our homes is borrowed up to the maximum at 10 to 15 percent interest. To pay for all this debt our wives had to work and our children became undisciplined. The children grow up and think nothing of both working full time earning just enough to make the payments on scores of expenses. Yes, the second and third generations forget. We repeat our mistakes. Had Christians been sensitive to the Holy Spirit when we would read verses in the Bible like "the borrower is servant to the lender" (Prov. 22:7;KJV) and others, we wouldn't be in this mess with our non-Christian countrymen.

From 1939 to the present, we've had about seven or eight recessions. There have only been two years (1949 and 1953) in which we've dropped into net deflation. The rest of those recessions have been inflationary recessions. So, as the cracks continue to spread in the financial system, watch for the Fed and the government to run the printing presses faster and faster and faster to try to inflate their way out of it.

The most likely scenario for our economy is the inflation-depression scenario. This is an economic condition wherein we have elements of inflation and deflation occurring simultaneously. Some prices will rise sharply and some businesses will boom; other prices will fall sharply and some businesses will collapse, all at the same time. Sometimes the balance of forces will be tilting towards inflation, sometimes towards deflation, and sometimes they will be temporarily in balance. Phenomenon of an inflationary recession or an inflationary depression is part of this scenario, like having the great hyperinflation of 1923 in Germany and the Great Depression of the 1930s all at the same time.

America is facing the greatest financial crisis in its history — far greater than in 1929. As a country, we, the government, businesses, and individuals have spent it all, and have gone on the most massive debt binge in history, adding about $14 trillion to perpetuate the facade of prosperity over the last 15 years or so. America is the world's largest borrower, and we're about to become the financial servant to our creditors: the world — spelled "The New World Order."

Several Options

If you don't want to get caught in this financial mire, here are some practical considerations.

Pray

First, pray. Confess that you have not been the

best steward of His assets. Ask forgiveness. Then ask for spiritual discernment for the future. Ask God to help you become spiritually, mentally, and physically strong to lead your family in these uncertain times. If you are not already doing so, every day you should read and teach your family biblical principals. Pray with your family on a daily basis. Pray for protection. Determine, through prayer and Scripture, how much you believe the Lord wants you to give your local church on a regular basis.

Change the Way You Think

Change the way you think about everything. We live in a different world today than you've lived in for all of your life. Change the way you look at and think about everything.

Invest in People

Be very careful about who you become close friends with. When you invest, you invest first and foremost in people.

Determine Your Strengths and Weaknesses

Determine your strengths and your weaknesses. Seek the counsel of others you trust to find out where your blind spots are. Learn to lean on your strengths and away from your weaknesses.

Eliminate Non-essentials

Eliminate non-essentials from your life. Analyze what is, and is not, essential. Determine what wastes your time and money — two very important assets that God has given you. Buy things that will cost less and last, even if they cost more now.

Develop Spiritual Discipline

Develop spiritual discipline. If you haven't already, begin memorizing Scripture and hymns.

Reduce Your Debts

Reduce your debts as quickly as possible and stay liquid. You can survive very tough times if you have little or no debt — this gives you tremendous flexibility. A lot of your assets should be in things that can be cash, cash equivalents, treasury bills, gold and silver, things that are cash or near-cash-type assets.

Save 10 Percent Per Month

Budget and save at least 10 percent per month. Avoid savings and loan deposits. Avoid all bank deposits over $100,000 in any single bank. For a lot of us that's a cinch; we don't even have anything like that. But for a few of you, spread it around, because there's no insurance to cover amounts over $100,000.

Reduce Real Estate Holdings

Try not to have more than 25 percent of your net worth tied up in real estate. It's illiquid, and in many instanceshas a lot of debt associated with it.

Avoid the Stock Market

Avoid the stock market unless you are a full time, moment-by-moment player. The little guy always loses. There are over 60 million people in the stock market now, more than any time in U.S. history. It's a ticking time bomb.

Avoid Corporate Bonds

Avoid all corporate bonds. I'm even a little bearish of U.S. government bonds. If you've got to have interest-bearing investments, research the possibility of spreading them over several currencies. It's a hedge against the U.S. dollar, and who knows where it will wind up.

Consider Precious Metals

Currently, most of the assets which we hold are paper assets, worth only what the supply and demand dictates. Consider putting a percentage of your portfolio in precious metals. I personally believe precious metals are going to do very well in the future. I would stick with U.S. gold and silver coins. They're more likely to remain legally tradable if the government ever decides to confiscate gold and silver bullion. Even if you have silver or gold coins, keep up to a month's expenses in cash at home.

Develop a Second Source of Income

Develop a second source of income, some kind of a small cottage business which you and your family might fall back on if you lose your job.

Develop Second Sources of Information

Develop second sources of information. Watching network television news and reading most daily newspapers will not give you an accurate and unbiased opinion of events. Many Christians haven't a clue as to what's really going on. However, there are available information sources to obtain a conservative biblical perspective such as private newsletters, Christian oriented newspapers, etc.

Again, continually pray for wisdom and guidance. You can make an incredible difference if you are armed with Scripture and the power of God. Proverbs

27:12 says, "The prudent see danger and take refuge, but the simple keep going and suffer for it" (NIV).

Some people say, "If you trusted God, you wouldn't think about such things as this. You would just pray." Well, I do trust God. But why did God instruct us to prepare for the future?

God has brought you onto the scene to live in the 1990s, to take a stand for the Lord Jesus Christ. Never, never give up!

Last thoughts . . .

God is, and always will be, in total control. Nothing is happening on this earth that He isn't allowing to happen. As Christians* we know how it ultimately ends — we win, they lose. Nothing will ever change that. But, as believers, we are commanded to "occupy" while we "watch." Maybe we will be fortunate and live long enough to personally witness the next major prophesied event, the removal of the Holy Spirit from the earth. Or, perhaps God will use people like us to protect our foundation so that future believers residing in the United States will have the same opportunities and rights we enjoy today. In any event, we'll be far better off STEELING our minds.

— Bill Perkins

*If you are not a Christian, or are not sure that you're a Christian, find a Bible and read the following New Testament verses in order: John 3:1-16; Romans 3:23, 6:23; Ephesians 2:8-9; John 14:6; Philippians 2:1-11; Romans 10:9-10; and 1 John 5:11-13.

NOTES

Chapter 1
[1]Mel and Norma Gabler, *What Are They Teaching Our Children in School?* (Wheaton, IL: Victor Books, 1985).
[2]Robert Dugan, *Winning the New Civil War* (Portland, OR: Multnomah Productions, 1991).
[3]James Dobson and Gary Bauer, *Children at Risk: Fighting for the Hearts and Minds of Our Kids* (Irving, TX: Word, Inc., 1990).
[4]John Eidsmoe, *Christianity and the Constitution, The Faith of Our Founding Fathers* (Grand Rapids, MI: Baker Book House, 1987).
[5]Dr. Ronald Nash, *The Closing of the American Heart* (Richardson, TX: Probe Books, 1990).
[6]John Ankerberg and John Weldon, *The Myth of Safe Sex; The Devastating Consequences of Violating God's Plan* (Chicago, IL: Moody Press, 1993).

Chapter 3
[1]Bill Clinton and Al Gore, *Putting People First* (New York, NY: Random Publishing, 1992).

Chapter 4
[1]Hal Lindsey, *The Late, Great Planet Earth* (New York, NY: Bantam Books).

Chapter 8
[1]Douglas Futuyma, from William J. Bennetta, "Scientists Decry a Slick New Packaging of Creationism," *The Science Teacher,* May 1987.
[2]Dr. Pierre Grasse, *The Evolution of Living Organisms* (New York, NY: Academic, 1977).
[3]Dr. Steven M. Stanley, *Macroevolution: Pattern and Process* (San Francisco, CA: W.M. Freeman, 1979), page 39.
[4]Dr. Wolfgang Smith, *Teilhardism and the New Religion* (Rockford, IL: Tan Books, 1988), page 2 and 5.
[5]Henry M. Morris, *The Long War Against God* (Grand Rapids, MI: Baker Book House, 1989).

[6]Isaac Asimov and Paul Kurtz, ed., "An Interview with Isaac Asimov on Science and the Bible," *Free Inquiry 2*, page 9.

[7]Henry Fairfield Osborn, "The Evolution of Human Races," *Natural History,* Jan/Feb. 1926, reprinted April 1980, page 129.

[8]Daniel Gasman, *The Scientific Origins of National Socialism* (New York, NY: American Elsevier, 1971), page xvi, xvii.

[9]James Rachels, *Created from Animals* (New York, NY: Oxford University Press, 1990).

[10]Andrew Carnegie, *Andrew Carnegie, Autobiography* (Boston, MA: Boston Publishers, 1920), page 327.

[11]Marilyn Ferguson, *The Aquarian Conspiracy* (Los Angeles, CA: Tarcher, 1980), page 50.

[12]Teilhard de Chardin, *The Phenomenon of Man* (New York, NY: Harper & Row, 1965), page 219.

[13]Teilhard de Chardin, *The Heart of the Matter* (New York, NY: Harcourt Brace Jovanovich, 1979), page 92.

[14]Elie A. Schneour, "Life Doesn't Begin, It Continues," *Los Angeles Times,* Jan. 29, 1989, part v.

[15]Henry M. Morris, *Biblical Creationism: What Each Book of the Bible Teaches About Creation and the Flood* (Grand Rapids, MI: Baker Book House, 1993).

[16]Alfred Russell Wallace, *The Wonderful Century: Its Successes and Its Failures* (New York, NY, 1898), page 139

[17]Loren Eiseley, "Alfred Russell Wallace," *Scientific American 200,* February 1959, page 81.

[18]Richard Wurmbrand, *Marx and Satan* (Westchester, IL: Crossway Books, 1986), page 12.

Chapter 9

[1]Al Gore, *Earth in the Balance: Ecology and the Human Spirit* (New York, NY: NAL Dutton, div. of Penguin, 1993).

[2]James Tyson, *Target America* (Washington, DC: Regnery Gateway Inc., 1981).

[3]Paul Boyer, *When Time Shall Be No More: Prophecy Beliefs in Modern American Culture* (Cambridge, MA: Council on East Asian Studies, 1992).

Hal Lindsey • As an internationally known lecturer and author of 11 books, including the runaway bestseller *The Late Great Planet Earth (27 million* copies worldwide!), Lindsey holds audiences spellbound on the subject of current world events and how they affect our lives. In the late 1960s Lindsey correctly predicted what would be taking place today through the study of Old Testament prophecies. He is considered one of the most respected and well-versed authorities this century on prophetic writings. He was named the best-selling author of the decade by the *New York Times*.

If you wish to receive more information on Hal Lindsey's books, tapes, magazine, or newsletter, write: Hal Lindsey Ministries, P.O. Box 4000, Palos Verdes, CA 98036, or call 1-800-TITUS-3-5.

Chuck Missler • He's been called the rising star of conservative Americans because of his combination of a long international business career, intricate knowledge of current events, and depth of biblical understanding. He rose from the Naval Academy to the upper levels of the corporate world and gained unparalleled insight and wisdom as to what is really going on from a global perspective. He recently switched from the corporate boardroom (serving on 12 public boards, 6 as president) to teaching the Bible. He has built a large contact network through his ministry, Koinonia House, enabling him to monitor the global movement toward a one world government and the implications for Christians in America. Missler has over *eight million* tapes of his Bible studies in distribution worldwide. His monthly newsletter reaches *over 50,000* subscribers per month.

If you wish to receive a free 12-month subscription to Chuck Missler's monthly Christian intelligence newsletter, *Personal UPDATE*, write: Koinonia House, P.O. Box D, Coeur d'Alene, ID 83816, or call 1-800-K-HOUSE-1.

John Ankerberg • Few people in America have impacted Christians as much as Ankerberg. He has authored or co-authored 39 books and is one of the Christian community's great apologists. Through his weekly award-winning television show reaching millions of homes he has meticulously exposed cults, false messiahs, government mis-information, false church leaders, and other topics that, left untouched, may have caused serious damage to the Christian community.

If you wish to receive more information on John Ankerberg, the Ankerberg Theological Research Institute, the John Ankerberg television show, or books and tapes available by John Ankerberg, write: The John Ankerberg Show, P.O. Box 8977, Chattanooga, TN 37414, or call (615) 892-7722 (8:30 a.m. - 4:30 p.m., ET)

Don McAlvany • For 17 years McAlvany has edited the *McAlvany Intelligence Advisor,* a geopolitical/financial intelligence newsletter analyzing global monetary, economic, and political developments and their effect on American lives. He is also president of International Collectors Associates, a 16-year-old Colorado-based precious metals brokerage. He recently authored *Toward a New World Order,* an eye-opening best seller exposing the behind the scenes orchestration to a one world government.

If you wish to receive more information on Don McAlvany, the *McAlvany Intelligence Advisor*, or his book, *Toward a New World Order*, write: McAlvany Intelligence Advisor, P.O. Box 84904, Phoenix, AZ 85029, or call 1-800-528-0559.

Henry Morris • As the founder and director of the Institute for Creation Research, Morris has steadfastly defended biblical inerrancy in *over 60* books on scientific topics. His classic titles, *The Genesis Flood, The Genesis Record,* and *Scientific Creationism,* are not only best sellers, but have also become must reading for serious Bible students.

If you wish to receive more information on the *Acts and Facts* monthly publication, *Days of Praise* quarterly devotional booklet, or the Institute for the Creation Research catalog of creationist books and videos, write: Institute for Creation Research, P.O. Box 2667, El Cajon, CA 92021, or call (619) 448-0900 or 1-800-743-6374 (voice mail).

Steeling the Mind of America Conferences

This unique conference is generally held every year in late August. Speakers for 1995 are monetary expert Larry Burkett, spiritual warfare expert Frank Peretti, political and prophecy expert Chuck Missler, apologetics expert John Ankerberg, Christian legal expert Alan Sears, environmental expert Edward Krug, and OBE/Goals 2000 expert Anita Hoge. If you want information on how to purchase audio or video tapes of past conferences or wish to be placed on the mailing list for information on future conferences, call or write:

Compass Conferences
3115 North Government Way, Suite 800
Coeur d'Alene, ID 83814
1-800-977-2177
fax (208) 664-1938